About the Author

After 30 years in Liverpool, where he was professor of vascular surgery, Peter Harris ended his professional life in London as a professor of endovascular surgery. This latter title reflected a career-long search for safer, minimally invasive surgeries in place of the bloody, high-risk operations that were the norm when he first started out as a consultant in 1979. He is now retired and lives in Devon and the south of France.

To my very beautiful wife, Carole, and to our three sons to whom I was an absentee father ensconced in hospital operation theatres for long periods during their formative years.

Peter Harris

No More Blood

A Life In Vascular Surgery

AUSTIN MACAULEY PUBLISHERS™

LONDON * CAMBRIDGE * NEW YORK * SHARJAH

A CIP catalogue record for this title is available from the British Library.

ISBN 9781528980012 (Paperback)
ISBN 9781528980036 (ePub e-book)

www.austinmacauley.com

First Published (2021)
Austin Macauley Publishers Ltd
25 Canada Square
Canary Wharf
London
E14 5LQ

When I first became a consultant, vascular surgical practice was essentially an individual endeavour. I was assisted by trainees but otherwise worked alone. That changed towards the end of the nineteen nineties for two reasons. First, it became widely appreciated that the physical fatigue associated with single-handed vascular surgical practice, with its heavy emergency out-of-hours workload, was actually dangerous to patients. Secondly, the arrival of minimally invasive image-guided interventions demanded a range of skills and expertise that could not easily be encompassed by one individual. The Endovascular Programme at the Royal Liverpool University Hospital, which was established in this period, owed its success then, and still does today, to a highly effective team of outstandingly talented individuals. I owe a debt of gratitude to those of my clinical colleagues who contributed so much to the setting up of this programme and with whom it was always such a great pleasure to work. They include; John Brennan, Rao Vallabhaneni and Richard McWilliams who are still flying the flag at, The Royal. And two team members who tragically died well before their time while still of working age; Geoffrey Gilling-Smith and Ali Bakran.

At the same time as minimally-invasive vascular surgery was taking off in the nineties, I worked with Abbas Rashid, a cardiothoracic surgeon at the Liverpool Chest and Heart Hospital, on surgical repair thoraco-abdominal aortic aneurysms. At the opposite end of the scale to 'minimally-invasive' this was very major high-risk surgery and, in our hands at least, it benefited from our combined skills of vascular and heart surgery. Being something of a colourful character it was always highly entertaining working with Abbas and we made a good team. The high profile that Liverpool still enjoys today for surgery of this type is down to Abbas's pioneering work and I was privileged to have played a small part in the success he achieved.

I would like to express special gratitude also to Thien How of the Liverpool University Department of Clinical Engineering. He and I collaborated on various vascular surgical research projects for more than 20 years. An enigmatic, deep thinker, he invariably came up with ingenious solutions to the engineering problems frequently encountered in the course of repairing or reconstructing blood vessels surgically. I not only valued his intellect but also his company and friendship.

Finally, as I write this, the Covid-19 pandemic is rife. I acknowledge and pay tribute to the courage and selfless work of all my former colleagues in the NHS and of health and social care workers everywhere as they respond to this crisis.

Prologue

This book is not about the NHS primarily. It is an account of the experiences, good and bad, of one individual who spent all his working life in it as a vascular surgeon. However, given that it is the constant backdrop to the events to be recounted, a brief historical overview here will set the scene.

The British National Health Service was created by the post-war labour government in 1948. Before it existed, doctors practised as private autonomous professionals, the only relevant contract being the, usually unwritten, one between doctor and patient. For a time, this almost sacrosanct relationship, the principles of which were defined centuries earlier by the Hippocratic Oath, were conserved within the new NHS. GP's and hospital consultants were not employees. They remained independent and contracted their services to the NHS thereby retaining control over the terms of their engagement with the NHS and their professional lives generally. The right to practice, without interference, according to the knowledge and beliefs inculcated in them by years of higher education, practical training and experience was not infringed. NHS administrators were relatively few in number and their remit was to facilitate the interaction between the doctor and the patient. The most senior administrator was not the CEO and he did not have an army of subordinates. He was the Hospital Secretary. If it was a big hospital, he might have a finance and a personnel manager to assist him. They had to balance the books but local medical needs dominated the agenda. Doctors, nurses and other professionals, allied to medicine, managed themselves.

The most important change effected by the NHS was to make healthcare for all UK citizens free at the point of delivery. For the first time, everyone had access to good healthcare irrespective of their financial means. Revolutionary at the time, and vigorously opposed by the medical establishment initially, this has been one of the factors that has characterised UK society throughout the world as decent and caring. This is how I found the NHS when I took my first steps into it as a medical student in Manchester in 1962. When I left it in 2012, NHS care was still mostly free at the point of delivery, but virtually, everything else about it had changed.

Hospital consultants had become employees with time-based contracts. They no longer had the freedom to practice according to their learning and experience, but were required to work within guidelines set by a governmental organisation called the National Institute for Health and Care Excellence (NICE). Performance targets that were, largely, politically motivated had replaced the needs and wishes of individual patients as a main focus of activity and doctors were no longer trusted to exercise control over their own professional standards. The main function of hospital managers, whose numbers had been increased vastly, was to ensure that government targets were met and 'short-termism', dictated by the interval between elections, outweighed long term healthcare planning.

In 50 years, between 1962 and 2012, successive governments, Conservative and Labour, imposed reorganisations upon the NHS with increasing frequency. Service improvement was always claimed to be the justification but invariably the true purpose was to cut costs. Adapting to disruptive change, over which we had little or no influence, would have been more acceptable to me and my colleagues had there been any evidence of clinical benefit. However, governments invariably failed to audit their own initiatives and what evidence does exist, indicates the opposite. In 2016, an objective study, published in the Journal of the Royal Society of Medicine* revealed a statistically significant, overall negative, impact of NHS reforms upon patient mortality. Moreover, as each reform resulted invariably in increased rather than decreased expenditure cost-efficiency must, in effect, have been reduced. The authors of this report concluded that *Politically led management changes to the NHS seem to be a wasteful ineffective practice.*

Despite the dubious impact of repeated government interventions, clinical outcomes within the NHS improved progressively over the years due to advances in medical science; that is until recently. For the first time in the history of the NHS, we have seen signs of this trend reversing.

Given the political and financial uncertainty prevailing today, it has been questioned whether the NHS can, or should, continue to be sustained in its present form**. The 70 or so years of its existence could turn out to be no more than a transient experiment in socialised medicine should it be concluded that it can no longer be afforded from tax revenues. However, this would almost certainly be a political decision rather than one engendered by unavoidable necessity. Some of its imperfections are apparent from experiences related in this book but I remain firmly convinced that its failings are massively outweighed by the benefits of treatment, free to all in need, at the point of delivery. With the necessary political will to make the financial commitment required, it remains capable of delivering the best standards of healthcare anywhere in the world and I believe passionately that the fundamental doctrines upon which the NHS is based are worthy of defence at any cost.

*Has NHS reorganisation saved lives? A CuSum study using 65 years of data. Lale AS, Temple JMF. Journal of the Royal Society of Medicine 2016; 109: 18-26

** Since writing, support for the NHS free at the point of delivery has been enhanced greatly following the Covid19 pandemic

Chapter 1
Tom Skully

It was five thirty in the morning on a wet Thursday in November 1992 and the streets of Liverpool were dark and deserted. Rain blowing across the Irish Sea on a cold north-westerly wind battered the buildings on the banks of the Mersey River. As I drove north along the dock road and away from the city centre, my headlights failed to penetrate the downpour and surface water concealed potholes in the road resulting from years of neglect of this once mighty port. On the side, away from the river, the occasional street lamp did little more than illuminate an encircling halo in the rain and there were faint glimmering reflections from the wetted brickwork and broken leaded windows of dilapidated Victorian warehouses. This was familiar territory and I was barely conscious of the surroundings or of my progress along the road. My mind was elsewhere. Not for the first time, in identical circumstances, I was deeply troubled by the events of the last few hours.

Five hours earlier, Tom Skully, taking advantage of a commercial break in the programme he had been watching on TV, had gone into the kitchen to make a cup of tea. Tom was of Liverpool Irish stock. Both his father and his grandfather had worked on the docks as casual labourers and when Tom turned 16, he left school to follow them. That's what you did in those days. But, the Port of Liverpool was already in serious decline and there were many days when he turned up looking for work and found none. In 1935, he married Eileen, his childhood sweetheart. He was 19, she was 18. They produced six children. When drafted in 1939, Tom elected to join the Navy and he spent most of the war years crossing the North Atlantic with the supply convoys to and from the United States. Many ships were sunk by German U-boats and many young seamen died. He was lucky. He survived unscathed. At the end of the war, he elected to stay on in the Merchant Navy and travelled the world as Able Seaman Skully for another six years. These were the best years of his life but by the turn of the decade, he had had enough and decided to return to 'civvy' life. He found a job as night watchman in a small factory in Bootle that made cheap furniture. But times were hard in Liverpool at this time, and in 1959, the factory closed down. He had little choice but to sign on the dole. He did casual work as a doorman or serving behind bar in various pubs and clubs, to supplement his dole money with ready cash. And, in 1979, his income was supplemented further by a disability pension, secured for him by a local firm of solicitors in the 'compensation' business. Merchant sailors using caulking hammers for chiselling rust off boats, and ship builders working with riveting guns and heavy drills at Cammel Lairds Shipyard in Birkenhead risked minor injury to the blood vessels in their fingers from the vibration. The result was a condition called Vibration White Finger Syndrome. It was annoying rather than serious, but the beauty of it was that the symptoms could very easily be exaggerated or faked and there was no reliable diagnostic test. Furthermore, it could be argued that those afflicted were no longer able to work with their hands and were therefore, denied further gainful occupation as a consequence of a failure of duty of care on the part of their employers. It was a lucrative business for some lawyers on Merseyside. Tom had responded to an advert on the local radio. His hands did not trouble him much, truthfully, not at all but on the basis of not looking a 'gift-horse in the mouth', he gladly accepted the hand-out.

Tom had just filled the kettle and was placing it back on its stand on the kitchen worktop when a pain, the likes of which he had never known before, struck him in the back. The next moment, he fell to the floor unconscious. Back in the front room, Eileen heard the clatter of the kettle hitting the lino-tiled floor. After marriage to Tom for the best part of 50 years, she knew to expect a string of expletives following a minor disaster of the sort that might be encountered during the course of making a cup of tea, but none such came. And she knew, right then, that something was seriously wrong.

The ambulance arrived within ten minutes of the 999 call and another ten minutes later, Tom was the centre of frantic activity in the A&E department at the 'Royal' as doctors and nurses strived to keep him alive.

At 12 minutes to midnight, the silence of my bedroom was shattered by the shrill ringing of the bedside telephone. I was instantly awake, heart thumping and in a cold sweat, like a startled animal. A telephone ringing in the dead of the night always meant trouble. Sometimes, it was minor and resolved with a quick

13

decision and minimum disturbance to the night's sleep. At other times, it was something else altogether.

There was urgency in the voice at the other end of the line; "Sorry to trouble you, sir but there is a man in Casualty with a probable ruptured abdominal aortic aneurysm." It was the resident surgical registrar on-call at the hospital for the night. Luckily it was my trainee and therefore he knew a bit about aortic aneurysms. His name was Mike.

"No trouble," I mumbled as I struggled to get my thoughts into focus, "Tell me more."

"He's a 69-year-old man, smoker but apparently in reasonably good health before tonight. He collapsed suddenly at home. According to his wife he was unconscious at first but he was moaning and moving his arms and legs a bit by the time the ambulance arrived. He is responding to his name now, but is very agitated and in a lot of pain."

"What's his blood pressure doing?"

"About 100 systolic at the moment. That's after significant IV fluid replacement."

"How sure are you that it's a ruptured aneurysm?" I asked, in the vague hope that it might be something else that could be passed onto someone else to lose a night's sleep over.

"Well, he has a history of two previous heart attacks. The last, about 6 months ago, but there don't appear to be any acute changes on his ECG to suggest a new myocardial injury. And we think, we can feel a pulsatile mass in his belly, although, he's a big man and very difficult to examine in his present state. There might be some aortic calcification on the abdominal X-ray also but it's a very poor image because he wouldn't keep still. Chest X-ray looks OK. His haemoglobin on admission was seven with a haematocrit of 36 consistent with a significant bleed."

Not much doubt about the diagnosis then. Resignedly, I scrambled out of bed and started to pull on underwear with my free hand as I gave instructions into the telephone "OK." Get some blood cross-matched, warn the operating theatre, and let the anaesthetists know. Give him a shot of morphine, if he is in a lot of pain."

Mike was already well ahead of me. "A blood sample is already in the lab. We've requested six units of blood and three units of fresh-frozen plasma and they should be ready in about half an hour. The anaesthetic registrar is here and he has called his consultant who is on his way in. And, I've checked; there is an empty operating theatre available."

"Good. I'll be there soon."

Twenty minutes is the time it takes to drive to the hospital from home when there is no traffic. You could do it in 15 if you put your foot down but I have paid fines for speeding *en-route* to emergencies at the hospital twice before – pleas of mitigation having fallen on deaf ears on both occasions. So, it takes 20 minutes.

I parked the car, illegally, in an ambulance bay outside the A&E Department and hurried inside. A nurse directed me to a bay in 'majors' where frantic activity behind the curtains betrayed the scene of a drama. Despite the morphine, Tom was in a state of agitated confusion trying to fight off the doctors and nurses who struggled to hold him down as he thrashed about shouting incoherently. There were drips running into his neck and into both arms. A cannula in his left wrist measured the pressure in an artery, a probe on his right index finger was recording the amount of oxygen in his blood and there were ECG leads on his chest. The outputs from all of these devices were displayed continuously on an electronic monitor which was beeping rapidly with his pulse. The rhythm was irregular. A tube in his nose was draining the contents of his stomach and a catheter led from his bladder to a bag hanging on the side of the bed, in which I noted there were a few drops of urine – a good sign.

There was terror in his unseeing eyes. His face was very pale and he was sweating profusely. I put my mouth close to his ear and with a voice as calm and reassuring as I could manage, I said, "Tom, we're going to help you. We know you're in pain and I promise we'll get you comfortable very soon. But first I want you to try to relax while I examine your tummy." Under the circumstances there was no chance of this but, in the brief lapses between his struggles, I managed an examination of sorts. He was a big man with a big belly. It was not only big but tense like a drum consistent with it being distended from within by a large volume of fluid under pressure. It was also extremely tender and he reacted aggressively as I tried to probe deeply. Despite the difficulties, I had no doubt about the presence, beneath his ribs, of a large pulsating lump that should not be there. Everything about him was consistent with the diagnosis of a ruptured abdominal aortic aneurysm with a belly full of blood.

The aorta is a high-pressure hose taking blood pumped from the heart and distributing it around the body. Tom's age, and no doubt, a certain amount of self-inflicted abuse including a life-time of inhaling tobacco smoke, had caused decay to the wall of the aorta in his abdomen and the pressure inside it had caused the affected segment, which was weakened as a result, to bulge like a balloon. Although unnoticed until tonight, when the balloon finally burst, the process of decay had been going on for years. Tom did not die instantly, because a thin membrane, the peritoneum, covering the front of the aorta had remained intact to contain, temporarily, the blood spurting from the rent. At the same time, his blood pressure had dropped catastrophically with the initial blood loss, to reduce the force of the leak.

The state in which I found Tom was not only transient but also extremely precarious. It was just a matter of time, maybe seconds, maybe minutes, an hour to two at the most, before the thin membrane compressing the haemorrhage would give way with instantaneous death. His one and only chance of survival was to close the hole in the aorta before the final *coup de gras*. But, that could only be achieved by major surgery in a man, well past his prime, and already close to death. It was a very high-risk option but since the alternative was certain death, I decided we must go ahead. The consultant anaesthetist was Jeff Lamplugh. Jeff and I worked together regularly and I knew him well. He was a very experienced cardiovascular anaesthetist and I trusted his judgement completely. He agreed, it's 'now or never', although just putting Tom to sleep was going to be a risky business, under these circumstances, never mind the surgery. He prescribed a drug to keep the blood pressure low with the aim of delaying terminal explosion of the aortic 'time-bomb' until we had Tom on the operating table and were in a position to attempt to do something to stop it happening.

I put my mouth to Tom's ear again and told him, "Tom, you're going to be fine. You need an operation to make you better. But, you're going to be fine. We're going to get on with it straight away." He was in no state to give 'informed consent', so I looked to find his nearest and dearest.

Eileen was sitting in a small room, down the corridor, some distance away from the hubbub of the emergency room. She was accompanied by her younger sister and by one of her daughters. I introduced myself and described Tom's situation as simply as I could. At the insistence of lawyers, patients or, as in this case, their legal representatives, must be informed of all the risks as well as the benefits of surgery. I decided to skip the finer details. I explained to her that Tom was very ill. That he had a chance of pulling through but only with a major operation. That we would do the very best, we could for him. But that we could not be certain of the outcome. With tearful eyes, she looked at me directly and asked, "Doctor, tell me honestly, what are his chances?" It is much easier to give unexpected good rather than unexpected bad news after the event and Eileen needed to be forewarned.

I replied, "I'm sorry, Eileen, even with an operation, they are no better than 50:50."

Then, she said, "And what will happen if he does not have an operation?"

"I'm afraid he will certainly die." I replied.

She turned to her sister and daughter, looking for guidance. They signalled their assent with their eyes and slight inclination of their heads. Then, Eileen turned to me again and wiping her eyes with a small handkerchief, she said, "Thank you, Doctor. Please give him a chance. I know you will do the best you can and we can't ask for more." I showed her where to sign her name on the form and then hurried off with it in my hand, down the corridor to the lifts. As I passed 'majors', I noted that Tom and his entourage of doctors, nurses, paramedics and porters had left already.

The operating theatre block is on the 12th floor and it took forever for a lift to arrive, as I watched the numbers changing slowly above the doors. Who is it, going up and down in the lifts, at this time of night? Eventually, when a lift did arrive it took me to the theatre level without stopping. I charged through the door to the surgeons' changing room, hurriedly stripped down to my underwear and donned green scrubs and white clogs. I tied a green plastic apron around my waist and grabbed a hat, and a surgical mask from cardboard boxes as I exited through the door that opened into the inner 'clean' area of the operating theatre complex. There was a long corridor with pairs of doors, leading into and out of twelve numbered individual operating rooms, along its length. Sounds of alarm emanating from number 8 indicated that things were not going well with Tom and I ran the last few paces before pushing through the swing doors.

Tom was on his back on the operating table. He was totally naked. Groaning and shouting loudly. Someone was hurriedly shaving his distended belly with a disposable plastic razor while someone else attempted to hold his legs still. At the head end, a young trainee anaesthetist stood on one side, squeezing blood from a soft plastic bag attached to the drip in Tom's right arm. On the other side, a nurse was squeezing a similar bag of clear fluid into the left arm.

Between them, Jeff was leaning over Tom's head. In one hand, he held the handle of a lighted instrument which he had inserted into Tom's mouth and in the other he had a long plastic sucker, which was making a loud noise at the back of Tom's throat. Frothy, green fluid was running along the clear plastic tubing leading from the sucker to a bottle mounted on the wall. Beside Jeff, on top of the anaesthetic machine, was a monitor which displayed ECG and pressure traces. It beeped in time with the heartbeat, which was rapid and irregular. The scrub nurse, Jan, was standing at the foot end of the operating table with a trolley of instruments covered with a green sterile drape. She was calling out instructions to her 'runners', junior nurses, who ran back and forth anxiously. Fully gowned and masked, she held in one hand, a small plastic pot containing an iodine solution and in the other, a pair of long metal forceps bearing a white gamgee swab. Mike, also gowned and masked, was standing beside her. Similarly attired, opposite him, was a young woman who I did not know. I presumed she was a surgical trainee, probably a senior house officer from another speciality. She looked worried and her face was very pale.

Seeing me, Jeff said, "Peter, we're in trouble. His pressure's dropping and he's having runs of supraventricular tachycardia. He's also vomited and he may have aspirated some of it, into his lungs. I'm going to have to intubate him right away, otherwise, we're going to lose him."

"Right," I replied, "Try to hold off a couple of seconds until I'm ready. I'll be there in two ticks." Turning to Mike I said, "Paint his belly and towel him up quickly."

There was no time to scrub properly. I pulled on a sterile gown and gloves in the scrub area and with a little junior nurse running along behind me, trying to tie the tapes at the back of the gown, I headed for the table. I noted the time on the clock, mounted on the wall in front of me; it was showing a minute or two after half past one. I surmised that the peritoneum holding back the bleeding had given way or was on the point of doing so. In which case, all that was preventing terminal catastrophe, was the pressure within Tom's distended abdomen contained by contraction of his abdominal wall muscles. When fully anaesthetised, all of his muscles would lose the ability to contract, including those of the abdominal wall and this very last defence would give way also. Therefore, only when fully ready, with scalpel in hand, did I give Jeff the nod to go ahead.

As the anaesthetic tube disappeared into Tom's windpipe, I incised along the length of his belly from the breastplate to the pubic bone skirting around the umbilicus. There was virtually no bleeding from the skin because his blood pressure was at or close to zero. Telling everyone to get ready with suckers, I made a hole in the muscle layer of the abdominal wall, just big enough to insert a couple of fingers. Bloody serous fluid jetted out through the hole under pressure and the suckers held by Mike and the young doctor, whose name I have determined is Susan, were completely ineffective to cope with the volume. The bleeding within, was now completely unrestrained through the rent in the aorta and Tom Skully's life was about to be extinguished within seconds. Jeff called out, "Pressure's gone and his pulse has slowed right down. ECG shows bradycardia." Taking a pair of large scissors from Jan, I slit open the rest of the incision completely. Bright red blood poured out followed by loops of distended slippery intestines and masses of jelly-like congealed blood. With my arm, elbow deep, within Tom's voluminous abdomen, I located the aorta by feel, worked my index finger and thumb around it then squeezed hard. At the top end, Jeff and his team were squeezing bags of blood for all their worth.

There was no discernible pulse initially but within a few seconds I could feel a feeble bumping against my fingers. The heart was still beating! After another few seconds Jeff confirmed that the cardiac output was picking up, with a blood pressure of about 60 millimetres of mercury. By now my fingers were aching and it was requiring more effort to keep the aorta compressed as the blood pressure increased again. We needed to replace my fingers with a surgical clamp. And, for this I needed to be able to actually see the aorta. Engulfed by masses of intestines and submerged beneath a pool of blood, which continued to well up from the depths, the aorta is encircled by big veins that are easily torn by a clumsily applied clamp. Getting a clear enough view was not going to be easy. But then, nothing about this whole business had been easy so far and desperate circumstances demanded desperate measures. With my free hand and with Mike's help I pulled all of the intestines out of the abdomen and onto my side of the operating table, Mike then inserted deep metal retractors over large gamgee swabs to hold aside the stomach and liver, while Susan did her best to clear the blood from around my fingers, in the depths, with a sucker in each hand. After several minutes of intense concentration, I had sight of the aorta and the vein to the left kidney crossing over it just above my fingers. "Hold still, everyone," I said. "I can see it," and, just at that exact moment, Susan announced she was going to faint. A nurse helped her from the operating table. She looked green. Jan took over the suckers and, after a few more precious seconds of straining in the depths, I spotted the vein and the aorta again. I freed the vein up and pushed it away with the tip of a pair of long scissors and then, without taking my eyes off the target, I helped myself to the longest arterial clamp on the instrument trolley with my free hand. Jan would normally have handed it to me but she was otherwise occupied. Mainly by feel, I eased the jaws of the clamp alongside my fingers, one side of the jaws on each side of the aorta and clamped it up. Mike pressed down on the handles to hold it firmly in place. Then, gingerly, I withdrew my fingers. The clamp held. Everyone breathed a sigh of relief.

With the worst of the bleeding controlled we relaxed momentarily. Jeff said he could do with a cup of tea. Jan said she could do with something a bit stronger and everyone else agreed. Then, we gathered together the intestines and pushed them back inside the belly. Now, even more distended than before, they won't all go back but what can be managed is an improvement on leaving them all hanging out. Meantime, the anaesthetic team are replacing more of the blood that has been lost. The six pints that were cross-matched originally had been used up long ago. They were well into the next six and had ordered six more.

"How's it going?" I asked.

"Well, he's looking a bit better since the clamp went on. Blood pressure's come up to 80 and his rate's 120 now but there are ischaemic changes on the ECG and he's getting occasional runs of ventricular tachycardia. Very unstable. He may have suffered significant myocardial injury. And, there's been no new urine, since we started."

In other words, the situation was grim. The bleeding was controlled, but there were signs that near zero blood pressure for several minutes, had caused further damage to Tom's heart and kidneys. This raised questions about his other vital organs, most importantly his brain. Also, with the aorta clamped, there was now, no circulation at all to his lower body and the tissues there, especially the muscles in his legs would start to decay unless the blood supply was quickly restored. Tom's chances of survival were decreasing by the second but, at that point, he was still alive and we had to go on. Mike and I, fastened a metal framework to the operating table to hold the retractors, so that we both had both hands free. We managed to pack away most of the intestines inside the abdomen behind the retractors and after a few minutes work we had a decent view of the aorta in the depths. We applied additional clamps to the two main branches of the aorta, the iliac arteries, to stop the last of the bleeding and isolate the aneurysm completely. I opened it up along its length with a scalpel. There was a large amount of thrombus inside it, which we scooped out with our fingers before stitching in place, a cloth tube of Dacron fabric. Joined with stitches to the normal aorta above and below the aneurysm and lying within it, the prosthesis would act as an inner tube to carry blood to the lower body. Reconstruction of the aorta in this way occupied another 45 minutes or so. Under ideal conditions, it can be done in less than 20 but these were not ideal conditions!

Finally, the job was done. Continuity of the aorta was restored. But the clamps were still in place and there was yet one more major storm to be weathered. In the absence of blood flow carrying oxygen to the cells, lactic acid accumulates in the tissues and this along with other noxious chemicals released by the breakdown of decaying cells, is highly toxic to the heart. In Tom's case, his heart was already damaged by what had gone before during the last few hours and the heart attacks suffered months or years previously. Removal of the clamps was going to bombard it with toxins and, at the same time, the blood pressure would plummet once again as the blood flowed once more into the lower body. This final obstacle to survival is known as reperfusion syndrome.

Having been there many times before, Jeff and I had a plan. He would top up the circulation with blood and give a bicarbonate solution to neutralise the lactic acid in preparation for the clamps coming off. When he was ready I would remove the clamps slowly by degrees to reperfuse first one leg and then, the other gradually and with a pause between while he stood by with syringes of adrenaline and noradrenaline to stimulate the heart should it fail. It usually worked but Tom was in a very bad way.

"OK," he said "Ready as we ever will be." I took off one of the smaller clamps; the one on the artery to the left leg. Nothing happened as there was not yet any blood flowing into the leg. Then I took hold of the handles of the clamp on the aorta and started to open it one notch of the ratchet at a time. As the blood began to flow we saw the Dacron graft open up and start to pulsate. But within a few seconds, Jeff called out, "Pressure's gone and I don't like the ECG!" I quickly clamped up again and felt the aorta above the clamp with my fingers. There was no pulse. "There's no cardiac output," I said in confirmation to the room at large and began compressing the heart intermittently with one hand outside the chest and the other, inside the abdomen under the diaphragm to pump the blood manually. After 30 seconds or so of this, Jeff said, "Stop a minute. I think we've got a spontaneous pressure trace. I stopped and we all looked at the monitor on top of the anaesthetic machine. There was indeed an arterial pressure trace with peaks of about 140 millimetres of mercury. The heart rate was very rapid. "I gave him adrenaline," said Jeff. "At least it shows, his heart is capable of responding."

"Shall we try again then?" I asked. "Might as well," he replied. And so, after more blood and bicarbonate solution, I opened the clamp again, very slowly. The pressure held for a couple of minutes this time and then dropped again precipitously. "Don't clamp him up again," Jeff suggested. "We'll just keep going through the reperfusion thing, again and again. Let's see what we can do at this end. He seems to be adequately filled, I'll try him with some noradrenaline and a bit more bicarb."

The heart made a valiant effort to respond once more, and the blood pressure started to increase again. Then, suddenly, the ECG trace switched into ventricular fibrillation. Cardiac arrest! I began cardiac massage again while the anaesthetic team prepared the defibrillator and attached the electrodes to Tom's chest. We gave him a shot, 20,000 volts. Initially his heart stopped contracting altogether. The ECG trace was a flat line. And then, after a second or two, infrequent bizarre-looking complexes appeared on the monitor. I felt the aorta again. There was no pulse this time. I started cardiac massage once more but it was apparent that the situation was hopeless.

I looked up and all eyes were on me. "What are the pupils doing Jeff? I ask. He quickly took an instrument with a light, off the top of the anaesthetic machine, pulled back the upper lid of Tom's left eye and moved the light back and forth across the pupil. Then he did the same to the right eye.

"Dilated and not reacting. Hard to say how much is due to the drugs we've given him but it certainly doesn't look good. Very probably, brain damaged I would say but I could give him another shot of adrenaline to see what happens."

Nobody spoke and I was uncomfortably aware that all eyes were on me again. I stopped pumping. "No Jeff. It's futile. He's gone." And then, "Sorry everyone. He's gone. We should not try to do more. It's time to stop."

Jeff nodded in agreement without saying anything and then, slowly and deliberately, he switched off the anaesthetic machine and the ECG monitor. The rhythmic, hissing noises made by the ventilator feeding oxygen into Tom's lungs and the beeps generated by feeble terminal contractions of his dying heart stopped and the room fell silent. "Thanks everyone," I said softly. "You all did a great job. It was not to be this time." The clock on the wall showed twenty-two minutes to five.

Then, the nurses set about clearing up while Jeff removed the drips, tubes and monitor leads. I was standing in a large pool of blood that was spread beneath the operating table and my lower body was soaked and my underwear was sticking uncomfortably to my skin. The plastic apron that was supposed to keep me dry had swivelled round to the side some time ago. I desperately wanted to change out of the wet clothes but it seemed unfair to leave the distasteful job of closing up the corpse to a junior and I told Mike to go and get a cup of coffee and write up the operation notes.

Closing up a corpse does not demand perfection. The pathologist would be opening Tom up again tomorrow in order to prepare a report for the Coroner. But, as a matter of respect for the just-departed, the job needs to be reasonably neat. The swollen, distended guts resisted being packed back inside and loops kept escaping. It took another 20 minutes before the job was finally done and I could leave the operating table. As I did so, Jan informed me that the swab and instrument count was correct; so, nothing had been left inside to attract the approbation of the coroner. I thanked her. As I departed the theatre, Tom's body was lying naked upon the table once more, as the nurses washed it down with large swabs and soapy water.

Back in the changing room, I stripped off the sodden theatre wear and removed also my underwear and socks, which I put in a plastic bag to take home. After a quick shower, I dressed in my outdoor clothes and entered the common room where Mike was still writing up the operation notes. He had made me a cup of coffee. It was cold so I made another. "Would you mind calling the Coroner's Office in the morning?" I asked. "There won't be any problem. There is certainly no doubt about the cause of death."

"Not at all," he replied.

"How's Susan? Has she left? Was she OK?"

"Yes. A bit shocked but she'll be OK. She left to go to bed about an hour ago."

"I guess Mrs Skully is still waiting in the visitor's room?"

"Not sure but the nurses will know, I'll ask them."

"No, it's OK, I'll ask on the way out. Thanks again Mike. You did well. Hope you manage to get some rest before clinic starts. See you tomorrow, or rather later today."

Eileen was sitting in a scruffy little room that said 'Visitors' on the door. It was on the 'dirty corridor' which ran parallel with the 'clean corridor' on the other side of the changing rooms. Her sister was sat on one side of her and the daughter who was there earlier, was on her other side. They had been joined by another daughter, who was about 35, and a son who was younger, probably in his late twenties. They all turned towards me as I entered. Trying not to betray too much too soon, I drew up a chair in front of Eileen. She grasped the hand of her sister on one side and that of her daughter on the other and looked straight at me with tear-filled eyes.

"Sorry, Eileen," I said softly, "We did the best we could." Somewhere behind me, I heard, "No. Oh, please God, no." And the young man started sobbing. The tears welled up in Eileen's eyes and she squeezed the hands holding hers. I felt my own eyes starting sting and there was a lump in my throat.

For a few seconds, I could not say anything. Then I swallowed hard and started again, "Eileen, I am very sorry. We did the best we could. We did manage to close up the tear in the blood vessel. But it was a very big operation. I'm afraid it was just too much for him. His heart was not strong enough."

For a time, it seemed forever, nobody said anything. Then the daughter behind me, stepped forward to hug her mother, followed by the young man and they all hugged each other. I sat there, not sure what to do. Eventually, Eileen turned to me and said calmly, "Thank you, Doctor, we know you did your best."

Then I said, "Someone from the hospital will be in touch with you in the morning to explain what must be done now. There are some forms to be signed." And with these incongruously banal words, I stood up and left the Skully family to their grief.

Driving home in the rain, northwards along the dock road, my mind was preoccupied with the disturbing events of the night and I found myself asking, not for the first time, "Why? There has to be a better way."

Throughout the 1980s and into the 1990s, there were many Tom Skullys, approximately 10,000 a year, in England and Wales. Not all died. Of those, who made it to the hospital and were operated upon, about half survived. But many collapsed and died before they could be admitted, often the true cause being recognised only at post-mortem examination. The true mortality rate was 90 per cent plus. There were very few recognised vascular surgeons at that time and, not unreasonably, most general surgeons, who were not used to operating upon the aorta, would not take on patients with ruptured aneurysms. Consequently, they came to my hospital from a wide area around Liverpool including Southport, the towns of North Wales and a large part of Cheshire. Two or three in a week was commonplace and two or three in a day or even in one night was not unknown. As real life and death emergencies, day or night, weekday or weekend, they had to be fitted in on top of the regular schedule of routine work. An uninterrupted night's sleep was a rare luxury in those days and I was chronically tired for years.

So, as I drove home through the wind and rain in the dark along the dock road that night, and on many similar occasions, I knew there had to be a better way. At that time I had no idea what that 'better way' might be.

Chapter 2
Time Expired

On another cold, rainy day 13 years earlier, at around lunchtime, I was standing in the entrance of a tawdry building on Old Hall Street in Liverpool City centre. It was February 1979. Half a dozen elderly gentlemen in grey suits had just interviewed me in a dimly lit basement room with a lino floor and trestle tables laid out in a U shape around a solitary hard wooden chair. It was a scene redolent of the interrogation of a WW2 spy in an old black and white movie. Evidently, I had impressed my inquisitors because they had offered me a job – that of a consultant surgeon at Broadgreen Hospital.

There was a payphone conveniently situated in the entrance and I called my wife Carole, at home in Sunbury upon Thames. "I got the job," I said.

There was a sharp intake of breath down the line, followed by a longish pause, then, "Oh!" Then another pause, followed by, "When do you start? When do we have to be there?"

"First of April, I replied, "We'll talk about plans when I get home." Another silence, then I heard her sobbing quietly.

Carole enjoyed her life 'down south'. She had made lots of friends and our three young boys were settled and happy in their school. She liked the proximity to London and did not want to move. The prospect of Liverpool, in particular, frightened her. Prejudices prevalent in the comfortable south east of England at that time were such that she could be forgiven for thinking she would find herself living among vagabonds and thieves in the midst of shabby, lawless, urban dereliction. Scousers were reputedly feral drunkards habituated to crime, violence, industrial strife and bizarre local politics. We were both brought up in the north but even other northerners considered Liverpool to be unflatteringly 'different'. We had been there, but neither of us knew it well, and our expectations were heavily influenced by these stereotypical clichés. It was definitely not the place Carole had wanted to bring up our kids and it had not been my choice either. So how is it that we ended up there?

Life began for me in Lancaster, 60 miles to the north of Liverpool, where I passed the 11-plus examination and attended the local Grammar School. I was not a model pupil. In the final year, I was one of only two boys in the upper sixth form, not to be awarded some sort of status as a prefect, a subprefect or even a monitor. Being singled out as unworthy individuals, David Shackleton and I took a perverse pride in not conforming and despised those who did. We adapted the school uniform to something more akin to our liking, best described as 'scruffy', and loitered at the margins of the social order being not so much antisocial, as indifferent to it. Despite developing a strong aversion to authority, I avoided getting into too much trouble and ended up with a decent set of 'O' and 'A' level examination results, a year earlier than most of my contemporaries.

I was most happy in the outdoors. As a kid, I was the Indian, never the cowboy or I was Robin Hood in Sherwood Forest. The idea of living in tune with nature had great appeal for me, and still does actually. After school and at weekends, I would spend most of my time wandering the countryside on my bike or fishing. For years, the only thing I ever wanted was to be a veterinary surgeon. Then, at the last minute, I changed my mind deciding that it might be more interesting to be a doctor. So, I applied to go to Medical School. My parents were ecstatic. My sister was a nurse but there had never been a doctor in the family before. Having rarely been anywhere south of Preston at that point in my life, Manchester was THE big metropolis and therefore, the obvious choice of university. London never crossed my mind, even less, Oxford or Cambridge. My application was accepted and I left home just a few days after my seventeenth birthday.

Initially, I lodged in a small terraced house in Old Trafford. One of my enduring memories of that time is of 'pea-souper' smog, so thick, you literally could not see more than a yard or two in front of your face. Recognising where you were, was not easy and I got hopelessly lost on at least one occasion, walking back from the university. After a few months, I fell out with the landlady. She was a fat lady with a dirty apron and curlers in her hair. She could have been the inspiration for Ena Sharples from Coronation Street. I was fascinated by a wart at the end of her tongue and could not take my eyes off it as it darted back and forth when she talked. One day she overheard me saying something unflattering about her to my fellow lodger and she threw me out with a week's notice. I moved into even less salubrious accommodation in a filthy basement flat in Moss Side that was occupied previously by a nightclub stripper. I went to look at the flat, with a fellow student who was also temporarily homeless, and she showed us a python which she used in her act and which she kept in a cage in the bedroom. It was not until my final year that I eventually got a place in a new University Hall of Residence in Fallowfield.

There were certainly some good times at university. I played rugby in winter and tennis in summer. There were social events at the Students' Union on Saturday and Wednesday nights with lots of alcohol and girls as well as many ad hoc parties but the grant I received was nowhere near enough to live on, let alone pay for beer and I hated asking my father for money. My parents lived comfortable enough lives but I must suppose that they did not have much money to spare because my father was not overgenerous. They were frugal times and I could not wait to qualify in order to earn my own money and become financially independent.

During the final year at medical school, students were attached to a clinical team for a few weeks to shadow the House Officer. The idea was to give us a foretaste of what to expect as infant doctors, assuming we passed the final examinations. By chance, I was allocated to the Professorial Surgical Unit at Manchester Royal Infirmary. And, it so happened that the Professor had a special interest in the nascent speciality of blood vessel surgery. At the end of the attachment, he called me into his office to tell me, "You must apply to be my next House Officer." On this occasion, I did do as I was told, and vascular surgery became my 'thing' for the rest of my working life.

It was a sunny day in June 1967, when the final examination results were posted on the Medical School notice board and I became a doctor. 'Whiter Shade of Pale' by Procul Harem was number one in the charts and flower power was in full swing as resistance to the American war in Vietnam gathered momentum. We grew our hair long and wore outlandishly flared pants. The Beatles' 'Sgt. Pepper's Lonely Hearts Club Band' was at the top of the charts and I duly became a house officer on the Professorial Surgical Unit at Manchester Royal Infirmary. My pay was £975 a year.

The professor's name was Michael Boyd. He was unwittingly hilarious. A bizarrely eccentric man, in the latter stages of his surgical and academic career. One of the rapidly dying breed of 'Sir Lancelot Pratts'. A chronic arthritic condition, called ankylosing spondylitis, had rendered his spine completely immobile, giving him, a humped back and he had to turn his whole body to look to one side or the other. Because his head was permanently inclined forwards, he peered over the top of his glasses through great bushy, grey eyebrows. He famously kept an irascible biting monkey in cage, at his home in Moss Side, and once surprised a burglar by shooting him with a shotgun from the top of the stairs. The burglar survived.

Although Professor Boyd was one of the first in the UK to specialise in vascular surgery, perversely, he believed that operating upon the blood vessels themselves, had virtually no place in the treatment of vascular disease. This was a theory, he spent most his academic life, trying to prove. He would have been a great asset as a surgeon in the Napoleonic wars because he prided himself on being able to take a man's leg off in seven minutes flat, using a large bayonet-shaped knife. There were actually, only three operations in his repertoire – amputation, sympathectomy and Achilles tenotomy. Of these, sympathectomy, in which the blood vessels in the legs are made to dilate by cutting the nerves that supply them, is now virtually never done because it has no lasting benefit. However, his most bizarre operation was that of Achilles tenotomy. This involved severing the Achilles tendon, which attaches the calf muscle to the heel bone rendering the muscle functionless. Patients, with impaired blood supply to their legs who previously developed pain in this muscle on walking, a condition called intermittent claudication, were cured of their pain because they were crippled and could no longer walk at all. Michael Boyd was the only person in the world, who thought this was a good idea. It was regarded by everyone else as the bizarre idiosyncrasy of a highly eccentric individual.

None of the Professor's operations, ever lasted more than ten minutes. The pain from his ankylosing spondylitis was such that he could not tolerate standing at the operating table for any longer. On occasions, this led to proceedings being brought to a swift conclusion, one way or another! Arthritis in his feet, added to his pain and he operated in a pair of 'comfortable', but none too clean, black gardening wellies. His approach to scrubbing up was 'unconventional'. It consisted of holding his hands under the tap for two or three seconds and then shaking them dry. I never saw him use soap. He wore his facemask under his chin rather than over his mouth and he would never wear a hat. The sterile operating gown barely covered his corpulent hairy body. As a result he bore an uncanny resemblance to Igor in the Frankenstein movie. Unsurprisingly, given his physical limitations, he undertook few operations himself, by the time I joined the unit and, fortunately for them, most of the patients were delegated to the care of other consultants who were more enthusiastic about the benefits of unblocking or bypassing blocked blood vessels. But a way had to be found to circumvent the professor's embargo on these procedures. The first step in planning surgery was an X-ray of the blood vessels called an arteriogram. In those days, this involved injecting a radio-opaque contrast medium through a long needle inserted into the aorta through the back – a procedure called 'Seldinger', after the radiologist who developed it. When the professor saw a new patient in the clinic, he would stamp the words 'NO SELDINGER' in big red letters, on the front of the case notes, to effectively exclude any possibility of surgery. Subterfuge with the cooperation of 'in-the-know', secretaries had to be employed to ensure that patients who seemed likely candidates for reconstructive surgery, were seen by someone other than the professor in the clinic without arousing his suspicion.

As it turned out, it was his opposition to surgical treatment of blood vessels that enabled Michael Boyd to make a valuable and long-lasting contribution to the science of vascular surgery and assured his place in history. He followed up all of his patients assiduously, recording what happened to them at regular intervals until they died. These records, then, formed the basis of a treatise entitled 'The natural history of vascular disease', which became recognised internationally as the standard benchmark against which all treatments, interventional or otherwise, for occlusive arterial disease could be compared to assess their efficacy. No one but Michael Boyd could have done this.

There was no European Union Directive on working time in those days. Being a resident house officer was a 24-hours-a-day, seven days a week job. You had to ask permission from your consultant, if you needed to leave the hospital at any time and you were expected to respond instantly to the beep of your pager, day and night. But everyone knew what to expect, and we were resigned to our incarceration, as a part of the process of initiation into medical practice. We were at everyone's beck and call from the junior ward nurse to the professor himself. At the start, young, inexperienced and totally lacking confidence in my ability to cope; I lived in a constant state of anxiety, bordering on panic. The telephone ringing in the dead of night was a major crisis. It could be, and often was, literally a matter of life and death. All new house officers are inevitably apprehensive but vascular surgery is a particularly high-risk speciality with more things going wrong than in other specialities. After being repeatedly terrorised by the telephone, in the middle of the night, as a house officer at Manchester Royal Infirmary in 1967, I developed an aversion to telephones, verging on phobia, from which I have never fully recovered to this day.

But it was not all work and no play. There were opportunities for pleasurable diversions. Alcohol was freely available in the mess bar and rules, excluding female visitors at night, were easily circumvented. Ad hoc parties happened often and 'formal' mess dinners, when it was obligatory to wear 'black tie', took place once a month. These were boozy affairs during which the mess 'president' would hand down 'forfeits' to people for spurious, 'breaches of protocol'. Generally, these were harmless pranks but when someone erected a wall, constructed of bricks and cement, across the main hospital corridor in the middle of the night, it had to be conceded that things had gone a bit too far.

Male chauvinism that prevailed at the time, was scarcely credible by today's standards. The doctors' dining room, an oak-panelled room with a long table, where we were served meals by uniformed domestic staff, was an all-male preserve at dinnertime. Female residents were served in an adjacent room. Although, I cannot remember anything at all about my bedroom at Manchester Royal Infirmary, I have vivid recollections of the bathroom. It was a magnificent relic of Victorian plumbing with a giant enamel bath standing on large brass claw feet set end-on to the middle of one wall from which big brass and enamel taps protruded. On pulling the plug, the bath water emptied into an open gutter that ran around the perimeter of the room and out through a hole in the opposite, outside wall.

The Reader on the Professorial Surgical unit and second in command was an anti-establishment, cavalier character called Ken Bloor. Having been a member of the communist party as student, he was barred from ever entering the United States, a distinction that he wore with pride. The surgical antithesis of the Professor, he was an enthusiastic operator who revelled in big surgery. He was adept at circumventing the 'NO SELDINGER' rule. Following the invention of heart-lung machines, he decided to extend his repertoire of vascular operations to include heart surgery. He was a heavy drinker, which probably accounted for a tremor in his hands that was particularly apparent during surgery. I marvelled that he could operate at all, but most of his patients survived. He had a cottage and a sailing boat in North Wales where he entertained the team to regular 'Vascular Unit Weekends'. These were immensely boozy affairs. Sailing or hill-walking was optional for those who were up to it, following the excesses of the night before. I cannot remember too much about the time I was included, but I still have a photo of me clinging to the forestay on the bow of the boat to prove I was there. Ken's girlfriend was called Val. She was the secretary to the professor, very attractive, full of fun and flirty. When Ken caught me snogging her at a party once, I was certain that my surgical career was about to be brought to an abrupt end. He warned me off in no uncertain terms but was probably too drunk to remember the incident afterwards and nothing more was said. Ken died prematurely, a few years later, from carcinoma of the oesophagus, most likely related to his heroic alcohol consumption.

The ward sister on the Professorial Surgical Unit was a fearsome Irish lady called Bridie Conran. I was terrified of her. She ruled with a rod of iron and, as the resident house officer, I was her whipping boy. The nurses on the ward were dressed in starched white aprons and had enormous white, lace-trimmed confections that were vestiges of medieval nuns' attire, on their heads. Any stray hair escaping from beneath these concoctions, or the slightest stain on an apron, would incur Bridie's wrath and everyone would know about it because her high-pitched Irish brogue carried a very long distance along the echoey hospital corridors.

The main event of the week was the Professorial Ward Round which Bridie stage-managed personally. It took place on Thursday mornings. The professor would arrive at 10 am with his entourage of consultants, readers, lecturers, research fellows, senior registrars, registrars, senior house officers and students. There was also a secretary to record his pronouncements in shorthand. By this time, the patients were sat to attention in beds, lined up perfectly down each side of the long open Victorian ward. Starched white sheets were turned back over the blankets and also aligned perfectly with those of the adjoining beds. I would be waiting, nervously, with Bridie and some of the more senior nurses at the entrance to the ward. It was my job, as house officer, to 'present' each patient to the professor. There were about sixty of them between two wards, male and female. The presentations had to be done without notes and woe betide me, if the professor requested to know the serum 'rhubarb' of a patient and I could not tell him off the top of my head. If I had omitted to do that particular test, it would induce a classical 'Sir Lancelot Pratt' moment. Having listened to the history, he would occasionally lift the bed covers to take a look at a black toe or to make some other perfunctory examination. Then, he would make an announcement, usually along the lines of, "Now, my man, you've got gangrene in your foot due to blocked arteries. The arteries can't be unblocked; therefore, we will have to amputate your leg. We'll do it tomorrow." And the entourage would move on. The patient himself had absolutely no say in the matter and usually responded with a meek, "Thank you, sir."

In 1971, four years after qualifying, I passed an examination to become a Fellow of the Royal College of Surgeons of England. I had continued to work in training posts, in and around Manchester, first as a senior house officer and then, as registrar in surgery. At the time that I passed the FRCS, I was a surgical registrar at Withington Hospital, which was shortly to become the University Hospital of South Manchester.

One of my consultants at Withington Hospital was a colourful character, who had a very big private practice in varicose veins. He wore smart blue suits, narrow blue ties and an ill-fitting ginger wig. His name was Sidney Rose. He was a director of Manchester City Football Club, which in those days was very much, second best, to the other Manchester team. On Friday mornings, Sidney had two concurrent operating lists, an NHS list at Withington Hospital and a private list at The Private Hospital. On both lists, there were private patients having operations for varicose veins. The one designated 'NHS' at Withington was delegated to me. Sidney would arrive at the hospital, first thing in the morning. Having parked his large blue Jaguar car in the 'No Parking' bay outside the operating theatres, he would slip off his shoes and pad into the anaesthetic room in his stocking feet. There he would pat the patient's hand as she – it was nearly always a 'she' – went off to sleep, telling her not to worry, he was there and everything would be well. As soon as her eyes were closed, he was off in his Jag to the private hospital where another patient was waiting in the anaesthetic room. I never saw a penny of the proceeds. Such was the culture at the time that neither I, nor any of his registrars, before or after me, thought to object. Someone did once have the temerity to suggest to Sidney that it might not be totally inappropriate for the registrar to receive some modest reward for operating upon his private patients. To which, he replied, "The reference I give you when you leave, will be more than adequate compensation." The converse implication, that failure to comply with his little scheme might be 'rewarded' with a bad, or no reference was lost on no one.

In 1973, I took a year out from clinical surgery to do full-time research under the supervision of David Charlesworth, a brilliant vascular surgeon who I first met at Manchester Royal Infirmary when I was a house officer and he was a surgical registrar on the professorial surgical unit. When humble Withington Hospital was upgraded to the grandiose University Hospital of South Manchester, David was appointed Reader in the Department of Surgery.

A year or two earlier, a device had been invented in Japan that had potential to replace harmful and dangerous invasive X-ray irradiation with harmless high frequency sound waves for investigation of diseased blood vessels. It had been found that ultrasound waves emitted from a small pencil-shaped probe on the surface of the skin would pass through the tissues and be reflected back again by flowing red blood cells inside an underlying artery or vein. The reflected sound waves were changed in frequency due to the 'Doppler effect' and because this change was related to the speed and direction of movement of the blood cells, it seemed possible that information may be deduced about the disease within the blood vessel. With the exception of the probe itself, my experimental apparatus was crude. Smoked paper on a rotating drum was used to convert the sound signals into visual representations, or sonographs and first, I had to create the smoked paper from sheets of white paper passed over a 'smoker', (a device containing smouldering wax that gave off sooty smoke to coat one side of the paper uniformly with carbon). The pulses or wave shapes displayed on the paper were traced onto graph paper and 'digitised' by counting squares. Finally, the numbers were fed into a computer, the size of a large wardrobe, with whirring discs and flashing lights, to analyse the shapes mathematically. In 1974, my thesis entitled 'The Role of Doppler Ultrasound in the Diagnosis of Arterial Disease' was accepted by the University of Manchester for a Doctorate degree. Today, the smoked drum and the wardrobe are obsolete, but ultrasound scanners with real time coloured images of blood flowing in blood vessels are the mainstay of diagnostic laboratories in departments of vascular surgery in all parts of the world.

With a fellowship and a doctorate under my belt, the Head of Department, Professor Ron Selwood, secured me a final training post as senior registrar at Charing Cross Hospital in London. The old Charing Cross Hospital opposite the station of the same name on The Strand had recently closed to be replaced by the New Charing Cross Hospital, a splendid glass and steel structure on Fulham Palace Road in Hammersmith. It was the NHS showpiece hospital of the day. Also, the first to be fully computerised with terminals on all wards, in the clinics and in the operating theatres for accessing laboratory results and X-rays. Massive computers with whirring drums of electromagnetic tape lined the walls of a large room in the basement and were tended by a small army of IT engineers. A steady stream of visitors from around the world came to marvel at the sight. In all probability, a small laptop computer would do the job today.

Initially, our family was accommodated in a high-rise residential tower block on the hospital site. We had two young boys at that time and Carole was terrified that one of them would fall out of a window; and, in any case, there was nowhere for them to play. So, we moved to Sunbury-on-Thames, a leafy suburb by the river about eight miles down the Chertsey Road from Hammersmith. We bought a small modern house there, with a little garden.

Ron Selwood had a friend who worked at Charing Cross Hospital and it was, in a large part, due to his influence that I got the job. He was a breast surgeon, so initially, I found myself examining and operating upon lots of breasts. Fascinating though, the human breast can be in certain circumstances; from a surgical perspective, I found it to be a relatively boring appendage. To pass the time, I embarked upon some research, specifically on breast 'elasticity'. I am not exactly sure how or why I chanced upon this topic but, intriguingly, I found that breasts with a propensity to develop cancer had less elastin in the tissue and were therefore, less 'elastic', i.e. less 'pert' than those of age matched controls without cancer. The clinical significance of this unique discovery was lost on everyone, myself included, and dismissed as irrelevant. However, my research into the elasticity, or 'pertness' of breasts added a few more publications to my CV, so it was not entirely wasted.

What followed was a lot more fun. In 1975, the training rotation took me to affiliated hospitals in Windsor and Ascot and I spent the long hot summer of that year, 'chilling' in the relatively relaxed ambiance of a bygone age. For time, it seemed, had passed by King Edward VII Hospital in Windsor and Heatherwood Hospital in Ascot. Situated, as they were, at each end of the 'Long Walk' in Windsor Great Park, along which the Queen, drives every summer in her open landau to see her horses' race at Ascot; they were a part of the Royal Windsor scene. The Royal residents of Windsor Castle did not patronise these hospitals themselves, of course, in times of need they use the other King Edward VII Hospital, the one for Officers in Marylebone, which is definitely not a part of the NHS. However, members of the Royal Household, maids, gardeners and the like, were admitted from time to time. One day, bounding down the main stairway, two steps at a time, at the hospital in Windsor I ran into Prince Charles, literally. His Royal Highness's bodyguard was quick to intervene.

It was my job to organise the surgery at these hospitals. I put together operating lists for the three consultants. It was made clear at the start that these lists should not include too many cases nor anything too big or complicated. There was more to life as a consultant surgeon in Windsor than operating upon NHS patients! I also put together operating lists for myself, that, force of necessity included big and complicated cases and I took care of all of the emergency surgical admissions. It sounds a lot, and I probably did work quite hard. For one thing, there were no other junior surgical staff sufficiently qualified to work on their own. This meant that I had to be resident, when on-call. King Edward VII Hospital in Windsor shared emergency responsibilities for the area with Wexham Park Hospital in Slough. Wexham Park was a bigger hospital with more staff, so they were on-call twice as often as Windsor. This still meant that I was away from home at least one night every week and one weekend in three. Not much fun for Carole, heavily pregnant and left at home looking after two mischievous little boys. I have to admit, I had the better of it, because at this particular hospital, mandatory internment had its compensations. For a start, it had an open-air swimming pool and that summer was exceptionally hot with seemingly endless days of sun. Having a quick swim or languishing at the poolside, I could see the rest room window of the operating theatre block well enough to be warned by appropriate signals from the nurses when the next patient was being readied for the operating table. In other respects, also it was a very privileged, old-fashioned, existence with 'hotel' service in the doctors' residence, which was called Demodra House. We luxuriated in three cooked meals a day in our own private dining room served by uniformed maids. Unimaginable today! While I took care of surgery in the hospital, there was another senior registrar who took care of internal medicine. His name was Sultan Shah. He was permanently resident. As far as I could tell, he had been living there forever and had no plans to move. And who could blame him. Because he was there constantly, it had become his domain. I spent a considerable time in his company that year. Fortunately, he was a genial, good fun, character and the time passed as pleasantly as possible under the circumstances.

Windsor is home to the Blues and Royals army unit and we used to visit the barracks across the road from the hospital to play squash. Just around the corner from these barracks, and immediately opposite the entrance to the hospital, was a pub called the Lord Raglan. After arranging with the ladies on the hospital switchboard for emergency telephone calls to be redirected to a number behind the bar, we would relocate there for a beer or two, during quiet periods, in the evening. At that time, the IRA had a nasty habit of bombing pubs, especially those frequented by soldiers, and the Lord Raglan was high risk. To keep the soldiers, and us, safe, the landlord invested in a set of heavy dark velvet curtains. We were not as convinced as he was that his curtains would impede the flight of an improvised explosive device, hurled through the window, sufficiently to prevent loss of life and limb, but we remained undeterred from our little forays to the pub. Fortunately, the effectiveness of the curtain strategy was never tested in anger.

The senior surgeon was called David Bain. He was a delightfully urbane gentleman immaculately dressed in tweeds and brogues, who drove an elegant Aston Martin car and lived in a fine Georgian terraced house, backing onto The Long Walk, on Sheet Street. He was the surgeon to Eton College, just across the river. For some reason, Eton College proved to be the source of an unusual number of teenage boys in need of urgent surgery for torsion of the testis. David Bain's anaesthetist was a decidedly eccentric character by the name of John D'Arcy. Dr D'Arcy was never seen without a cigarette in his mouth. He smoked in the changing room, in the coffee room, in the anaesthetic room and in the operating theatre. He usually had at least three patients asleep at any one time – one waiting to be operated upon, another being operated upon and the third recovering from being operated upon. This was a very efficient system which ensured that operating lists always finished on, or before, time. But, with so much oxygen and other explosive vapours about in the operating room, the chances of us being blown to bits in the process must have been considerably higher than they were in the Lord Raglan from an IRA bomb.

Heatherwood Hospital down the road at Ascot was a haven for bunny rabbits, their little white tails bobbing in front of you along the hospital corridors. Like many hospitals in Britain, it came into existence in Victorian times as a TB sanatorium with individual pavilions connected by an open corridor. Fresh air was thought to be good for the afflicted and it was considered, not unreasonably, that the open spaces would reduce the risk of cross-infection. With the exception of a new maternity block, very little had been done to it since those days. It still consisted of single-storey pavilions connected by open corridors. It was really a cottage hospital where patients were sent to convalesce or die, but it had a small operating theatre for minor surgical procedures such as hernia repairs and haemorrhoidectomies. I operated there once a week on Thursdays. One night, when I was on-call at Windsor, a man turned up at Heatherwood with a ruptured aortic aneurysm. He was far too unstable to be transferred anywhere and I decided to give surgery a go, rather than stand by and watch him die. He survived. It was a first and a major revelation for little Heatherwood Hospital.

The new maternity unit was set apart from the old hospital complex. It was a bright modern building with views overlooking the enclosures at Ascot racecourse. Carole gave birth to our youngest son there on 15th October 1975.

The year at Windsor and Ascot passed very quickly and then it was back to the future at Fulham Palace Road in West London where, at last, I was assigned to vascular surgery. At Charing Cross Hospital, this was a function of the professorial surgical unit. The head of department was Professor Harding Rains, who I held in great awe, because he wrote, or at least edited, the standard surgical textbook which I, and every other surgeon of my era, relied upon when studying for the Fellowship Examination of the Royal College of Surgeons. He was at the end of his career and within six months of my arrival on the unit, he retired. Although, my academic portfolio hardly matched professorial standards and I was just 32, I was encouraged to apply and thought I should show willing. Having had no expectation of success I was surprised to find myself on the short list. The only other candidate shortlisted was a senior lecturer in surgery from St. Barts Hospital in northeast London called Roger Greenhalgh. He was a well-connected, high-flying, academic and naturally enough, he got the job. It had, of course, been a foregone conclusion and my inclusion had been only to give the illusion of fair competition. That was OK with me. He was, undoubtedly, the better candidate and I bore no grudges.

A few months later, Roger began work as the new professor and as the incumbent senior registrar on the unit, he was my new boss. I tried to be helpful but it soon became apparent that he wanted me out of the way. After a very brief honeymoon, there followed a series of rows, the most serious of which related to the provenance and ownership of a research project that I had been engaged upon ages before his arrival. I decided I had to move and requested a transfer to cardiac surgery. My request was granted and I was glad to get out.

Charing Cross Hospital was not noted as a major centre for cardiac surgery being dependant, as it was, on just one consultant who also did general surgery. The consultant's name was Arthur Makey. He was a very modest, quietly spoken, man. Tall and thin with delicate hands and fingers, he was a good surgeon but his efforts were vastly overshadowed by those of internationally renowned heart units in the neighbouring Hammersmith and Brompton Hospitals. Harefield Hospital, home of the celebrated cardiac surgeon Magdi Yacoob was not too far away either. Consequently, relatively few patients came to Charing Cross Hospital for heart surgery. There was just a slow trickle of patients referred by the cardiology department in the same hospital. The senior registrar in cardiology was an engaging and very enterprising Australian called Keith Woolard. He was equally frustrated with the slow pace of life and with that in common, we came up with a scheme for generating more work. In the event, it turned out to be so successful that the workload got totally out of hand and brought me, literally, to my knees. The third person involved in this venture was Alberto Bartoli, the Italian pump technician who managed the heart-lung machine for open-heart operations. Alberto was an extrovert character who threw himself into the venture with typical over-the top Italian pazzazz.

It was 1977, and a new mechanical device, called an intra-aortic balloon pump, had just been invented. Inserted into the aorta, close to the heart, it helps to pump the blood in patients whose own heart is failing. There was good evidence already that it was effective but its precise role in clinical practice was uncertain and at that time, there were very few available. Today, intra-aortic balloon pumps are standard equipment in every cardiac surgery unit in the world. The balloon itself is small enough to be inserted into the patient through the femoral artery in the groin but the machinery that generates the pressure and controls the timing to coincide with the heartbeat is the size of a medium sized cabinet. With the aid of a research grant, we managed to acquire four intra-aortic balloon pumps and an ambulance. We then offered a service to the neighbouring hospitals in West London whereby we would arrive in the ambulance to hook-up a patient in heart failure to an intra-aortic balloon pump and bring them back to Charing Cross Hospital for further tests and definitive treatment.

We learned a lot about the use of intra-aortic balloon pumps. The most important lesson was that if heart failure had a mechanical cause, such as a hole in the heart or a leaking valve following a heart attack, which could be corrected surgically, lives could be saved. However, if the heart muscle itself was irreparably damaged, the balloon pump was capable of reviving the patient only so long as the machine was working. In these circumstances, there was nothing to be done other than to switch it off and let the patient die. One group of subjects, who did particularly well, were those with 'crescendo angina' which occurs when a heart attack evolves progressively over a period of time. The intra-aortic balloon pump effectively stopped the process in its tracks and then, when the underlying blockage in the coronary artery had been treated surgically, the patient usually recovered completely without suffering any permanent damage to their heart. We wrote up our results on this group of patients for publication in a scientific journal.

Problems arose because the uptake of our service far exceeded expectations. We were a unique three-man team and there was no one else in the hospital willing or able to lend a hand. Effectively, we were on-call 24 hours a day, 7 days a week and, although, well rewarded financially, there was absolutely no respite. Eventually, the strain got to me. One day, after arriving home from operating in the early hours of the morning, I suddenly felt lightheaded and collapsed to the floor. When I came around, I was in a panic, certain that I was haemorrhaging internally and I got myself admitted to the hospital by emergency ambulance. All blood tests and X-rays were completely normal. I was just exhausted.

On 1 April 1978, I became what is known as a 'time-expired' senior registrar. That is to say, my time as a trainee was up. For the training system to work as intended, completion of the four-year senior registrar programme should be followed quickly by appointment to a definitive consultant's post in order to vacate the position for the next in line. The trouble was that someone in the Department of Health had either got their manpower calculations wrong or, more likely, had deliberately manipulated the numbers to exert downward pressure on salaries. Whatever the reason, in the late 1970s, there was a considerable number of 'time-expired' senior registrars chasing a dearth of consultant jobs and the whole system became clogged. In more equitable times, you had a certain amount of choice regarding the type of hospital and the area of the country where you ended up in a consultant post. Not unreasonable, given that, that is most likely where you will be spending the rest of your life. Those in charge of these matters decided to unclog the system by denying choice. I was given a temporary contract for six months and told that at the end of this period, if I had not secured a consultant job, I would have to appear before a committee to explain why. Renewal of the contract was conditional upon my demonstrating that I had applied for every vacancy for which I was qualified, irrespective of the type of hospital or its location. The first job to come up was in Guildford. A very nice hospital, in a very nice town close to London. It would have suited us perfectly. However, despite flying home from a holiday in Corsica to attend a 'trial by sherry', some weeks prior to the formal interview, I failed to get the job. Arthur

Makey obviously felt sorry for me because he reimbursed me the cost of the airfare in return for operating on his varicose veins. It was a good deal for him – he had very bad varicose veins! St Mary's Hospital in Paddington was next. Felix Eastcott who was the best-known British vascular surgeon of his generation was retiring. I applied and was short-listed again, but I knew nobody at St Mary's, and without the right contacts I was not in with a realistic chance. It was a good interview but, as expected, the job went to the local candidate. And then, an advert appeared in the British Medical Journal for a consultant vacancy in Liverpool. Not at the Royal Liverpool University Hospital, which would have carried some cachet at least, but a small district general hospital I had never heard of, somewhere in the eastern suburbs of the city called Broadgreen. On this occasion, I did get the job.

Chapter 3
Terry, Eileen, Tommy, Derek and Annie

As I sank back into a chair in the theatre rest room, Thelma handed me my seventh or eighth mug of coffee of the day. I had lost count. Thelma was the domestic help in Unsworth Theatres at Broadgreen Hospital. It was her mission to make sure that I was never without a cup of coffee, when not actually operating. It was 7.30 in the evening and I was sick of the taste of coffee but, not wanting to appear ungrateful, I thanked her and took a sip. It had been a typical operating day at Broadgreen Hospital in the mid-1980s.

Thelma was in her late 40s but a lifetime of 'ciggies' and living alone in a small inner city Liverpool flat had aged her beyond her years. Gaunt with dry, straw-coloured hair, she had a strong scouse accent and a sardonic sense of humour. Every situation provoked a quip. She was particularly scathing about individuals she did not like, of whom there seemed to be many. "Proper divvied 'e is. Does me 'ed in," was her standard gibe. I was lucky; I was 'boss', which was not to say I was THE boss but about as high up on Thelma's scale of approval as it was possible to get. From time to time, she would show me photos of her, one and only living relative, a brother who had emigrated to Australia in the early 70s. As far as Thelma was concerned, he might just as well have emigrated to another planet. She was resigned to never seeing him again. Her only 'family' was a small mongrel dog left on its own all day to 'guard' her little flat.

In the mid-80s, there was no shortage of work for a vascular surgeon in Liverpool. The traditional lifestyle of Scousers strongly predisposed them to vascular disease and there were few of us to take care of them. There was, and still is, a view that prevailed in some better off parts of the Country that the hardships endured by Scousers are largely self-inflicted and that they 'get what they deserve'; that is to say, not very much! This mindset was exemplified by the scarcely believable and utterly disgraceful cover-up after 96 Liverpool football fans died as a result of police incompetence at Hillsborough football ground in 1989. Today health care resources are distributed more equitably across the Country than they were then but, at that time, the contrast between the 'have's' in the southeast of England and the 'have not's' in Liverpool was stark, not least in respect of vascular surgery. Before my arrival, in 1979, there had been just three vascular surgeons serving greater Merseyside, the whole of North Wales, North West Cheshire, The Wirral, Southport and West Lancashire. One, who I replaced was based at Broadgreen Hospital, and the other two at the Royal Liverpool University Hospital. Within a short time of my arrival in the City, both surgeons at the Royal had departed and the 'powers that be' decided that two in one hospital was too many and that only one would be replaced. Unfortunately, within a short time the individual concerned found himself out of his depth and unable to cope. To give him credit, despite his discomfiture, he did hang on doing the basics for almost 10 years, but there were rumours of heavy drinking and less-than-ideal clinical outcomes. Then one day, with no warning, he simply failed to turn up for work and was never seen again. Consequently, there were long periods in the 80s and early 90s, when I was Liverpool's only, fully functioning vascular surgeon to serve a population of almost two million people. The upside of this was that I attained prodigious experience within a very short period of time. The downside was that I was seriously overworked.

My fallibility as a surgeon was cruelly exposed at times especially early on in my consultant practice. I learned mostly from making mistakes. By and large Scouse patients are exceptionally trusting and tend to accept bad outcomes fatalistically without seeking to apportion blame, but my conscience was often gravely troubled. What also became very apparent to me during this period, were serious limitations of many of the accepted standard vascular operations that I had been taught during my training. This led me to *ad hoc* surgical experimentation in a way that would be impossible today. Not for a minute would I try to defend this as an acceptable way of doing things now, or indeed then, but at the time it seemed entirely appropriate given the often-tragic consequences of the failures which were painfully apparent to me. It never occurred to me that anybody could conceivably consider that what I was doing was in any way unethical and I rarely troubled the hospital ethics committee.

Thelma had handed me my first coffee of the day in the theatre rest room shortly after 8.00 am as I reviewed the notes of the first patient to be operated upon that day. Terry was a 49-year-old supervisor at Fords motor factory in Halewood. He had had increasing difficulty walking for a couple of years. After going for a few minutes, his legs would become painful and eventually he would have to stop and rest. The pain soon settled but the distances he could manage between stops were getting progressively shorter and he was not sure for how long he would be able to keep working if things got much worse. Actually, had it not been for something else, he would have put up with the pains a bit longer. What actually took him to the doctor did not seem related in any way to the pains in his legs. To his great consternation, he had found that he could no longer get an erection. The pain in his legs, he could have put up with. His sex life was another matter altogether.

Tests showed that the aorta in his abdomen was totally blocked. As a consequence both of his legs, and his genitals, were deprived of an adequate blood supply. In the 1980s surgical bypass of the blockage was the only effective treatment option and it was this or nothing. Actually nothing was often the best option given that the surgery carried serious risks. I operated upon several people with blocked aortas every week throughout the '80s and had a well worked out technique. Even so the mortality rate was around five per cent.

Sex is a complicated business and it was the case that restoration of erectile function could not be guaranteed, which for some, was just as important a consideration. Fully informed consent was clearly essential. Terry was not deterred by the statistics. As far as he was concerned, if there was a reasonable chance that his virility would be restored it was definitely worth taking the risk, and a 95 per cent likelihood of survival seemed like good enough odds in any case. If he could walk again without discomfort and continue working it would be an added bonus.

By 8.30 am, he was unconscious on his back on the operating table. His entire body was covered by sterile green drapes apart from a window of clear plastic adhesive sheeting over his abdomen and groins. As I entered the theatre my senior registrar at the time, a mild-mannered Scot named Hector Campbell, was standing masked and gowned by the side of the table with Carol, the scrub-nurse, next to him. A young, Indian Senior House Officer, also scrubbed and gowned, was hovering in the background, uncertain where to put himself, and a couple of junior nurses in theatre greens were busying themselves in response to Carol's instructions. A transistor radio, perched on a trolley next to an assortment of packs of sterile instruments wrapped in buff-coloured paper, was playing smooth oldies on Magic 98.4 FM. Two suckers, connected by clear plastic tubing to bottles on the floor, were hissing softly. Jeff, the anaesthetist, was sitting at the head of the table amidst various wires and tubing connected to his anaesthetic machine. He filled in details on a chart and adjusted the drips from time to time.

This was my domain; a peaceful haven and an escape from the hurly burly of the outside world. I wanted to keep it that way. Tension in operating theatres makes people stressed, unhappy and inefficient. Relaxed concentration is what is needed. So, we listened to the radio and chatted about this and that, as we worked our way into Terry's body.

Starting in the groins I worked on one side and Hector on the other to expose the femoral arteries. Then we made a long incision across the abdomen from one side to the other, just above the umbilicus. An incision we labelled the 'Broadgreen Smile' for reasons that can probably be imagined. With stainless steel retractors inside, to hold the guts out of the way, the aorta was visible in the depths. The retractors were anchored to a scaffold attached to rails on each side of the operating table so that we all had our hands free for other things. There was strong pulsation in the upper part of the aorta, but lower down, it was completely solid. The blockage started just below big branches coming off on each side of the aorta to supply the kidneys. Sufficient blood was reaching Terry's lower body to keep it ticking over because small branches that normally supply blood to the tissues locally above the block had joined with similar small branches arising below the block and enlarged to make a series of natural bypasses. It was like a blocked motorway with traffic piled back to an exit into which some vehicles are able to escape to join diversions along minor roads. Everyone reaches their destination eventually but only after a long delay. We could have attempted to unblock the aorta but this was technically more difficult and therefore more dangerous than the alternative of creating a new 'aortic motorway'. This entailed stitching in place a substitute aorta in the form of a pair of trousers made from Dacron (a biologically inert polyester) fabric. First we stitched the body of the trousers to the aorta above the block then threaded legs through the pelvis to the groins for attachment to the femoral arteries. With all three joins completed; the clamps, which had to be applied to stop the blood flowing while this work was done were removed and a full force of blood flowed once more into Terry's lower body. Jeff burrowing under the sterile drapes at the bottom of the operating table confirmed that pulses had been restored to the feet.

Half an hour later, all incisions were closed and dressed and Terry was waking up.

In the rest room, Thelma handed me another cup of coffee as I wrote up the operation notes. Then there was just time for a quick look at the back pages of last night's Echo before the next patient. Liverpool Football Club was proving to be just as unassailable under Joe Fagan as it had been under Bob Paisley. In 1983, the Reds went on to win three titles, the football league, the European cup and the league cup. Thelma was a massive fan. She was "Well made up" when they won and "Got a real cob on" on the rare occasions, when they lost.

Next on the table was Eileen. She was 62. She had been a worker at the Tate and Lyle Sugar Refinery in Liverpool's Love Lane for many years. That was before European Economic Community regulations favouring European sugar beet over Caribbean sugar cane closed it down. Spirited protests under the slogan 'Beat the Beet and Keep the Cane' by the 'Boys and Girls from the Whitestuff', as Tate and Lyle workers were known, had been to no avail. Through no fault of her own, and certainly nothing to do with the fact that she had worked in a sugar factory, Eileen was diabetic. Amongst other complications, this caused the arteries in her legs to fur up. She had had no inkling of this until one night when she happened to stub her big toe, stumbling to the toilet in the dark. It had been a very minor knock and she had thought nothing of it but, a few days later, the toe was red and angry and the tip had turned black. She had no pain because the diabetes had damaged the nerves to her feet and she couldn't feel anything at all. Eileen had diabetic gangrene and the whole of her limb, not just the toe, was at risk. All the arteries in her lower leg were blocked but an X-ray showed one still open in the groove behind the bone on the inside of her ankle. This was the only remaining source of blood supply to the foot. It was tiny with a diameter of about one millimetre.

A bypass onto this small artery was possible and might save her leg but it was going to be difficult and success could not be guaranteed. The alternative was to amputate the leg below the knee. In Eileen's mind, she was not at all sure that death would be a worse outcome than amputation. She lived alone and did not see how she could possibly manage, with only one leg.

The sort of bypass that was best for Eileen, was one constructed from her own natural blood vessels. There were artificial grafts available but they had little chance of working joined to such a small artery so far down the leg.

Arteries carry blood into the leg and are limited in number. Veins return the blood out again, towards the heart and are plentiful. It is unclear why, but nature has furnished humans with a surplus of veins; it is a happenstance that comes in very handy in Eileen's circumstances. There is a long vein that runs from the ankle all the way back to the groin. It is the one that is often stripped out in patients having operations for varicose veins operations and it is not missed. It makes a very effective 'spare part' for replacement of blocked arteries.

However, there is a major problem associated with using veins to replace arteries. They have valves whereas arteries do not. The function of the valves is to ensure that blood can flow through the vein in one direction only, out of the leg and back to the heart. This is necessary because, in contrast to arteries, through which blood is pumped, blood flows in the veins under very low pressure and without valves it would simply flow back again, down the leg, every time we stand up. A simple solution for overcoming the inconvenience of the valves is to take the vein out of the leg completely and to put it back upside down before connecting it to the artery as a bypass.

It is an intricate, fiddly, job and not one to be rushed. So, with Magic FM playing softly in the background, I settled comfortably onto a stool beside Eileen's leg. Two hours later, the last of the clamps were removed and the foot flushed pink and warm again, as blood flowed into the foot under pressure once more. The graft might not last forever but, if it stayed open long enough for the toe to heal, there was a chance, if she was lucky, that the leg would be alright even if it was to fail later. And, that would be more than good enough as a result.

Half of all of the long bypasses I carried out in patients with gangrene were failing within a year in the 1980s. And, despite our hopes for Eileen, failure made amputation inevitable for most. The suffering experienced by these patients was horrendous and made me acutely aware of my limitations. Sometimes progression of the underlying arterial disease was the cause but this did not seem to account for the majority. Veins are delicate complex structures and there is no doubt that the surgical trauma of taking them out of the body and putting them back in again sometimes compromised their ability to keep functioning despite my best efforts to handle them gently. Years earlier a different solution to the problem of valves had been proposed. It involved leaving the vein where it was, *in situ*, and cutting out the valves. The idea did not take off because there are many valves and to expose and excise each one, with multiple incisions into the vein, inevitably caused more damage than taking the whole vein out and reversing it. Then, in the early 80s someone invented a valve cutter. An instrument that could be passed up inside the vein on the end of a long wire to cut the valves from the inside. In theory, if it worked, there would be no need to expose the vein at all, except at each end, where it would be joined to the artery. It seemed too good a solution to be true - and it was. When I tried it out first at Broadgreen Hospital, I soon discovered that it was not such a simple solution as it seemed. The cutter did not always cut the valves reliably but the main problem was that branches joining the vein back-filled with arterial blood once the graft was joined up and this caused serious complications. It soon became clear that all of these branches would have to be tied off, which would mean either the whole length of the vein would have to be exposed or repeated X-rays taken on the operating table to locate them and lots of separate skin incisions made over each one.

Despite the drawbacks many vascular surgeons around the world, probably the majority, were persuaded that the new '*in situ*' operation was better. I was unconvinced and decided to undertake a trial to compare the two techniques on our patients at Broadgreen Hospital.

Although prospective randomised trials had been the well-established 'norm' for testing new drugs for many years, they were not generally considered applicable to surgical procedures. A new tablet could be tested against an identical-looking placebo so that neither the patient nor the doctor knew which was being administered in a way that eliminated bias completely. Clearly, it was not possible to do a 'double-blind' trial in surgery but as I genuinely did not know which of two techniques was better; it seemed perfectly reasonable, and ethical, to select patients for one operation or the other on a random basis and then to compare the results in the two groups. There was a 'hard' non-subjective end-point; the graft either stayed open or it blocked. It was black or white, open or closed, with nothing in between, so interpretive bias would not be an issue. All variables other than the operative procedure itself, would be eliminated so it seemed to me to be an entirely objective and valid way of deciding what was best for my patients. And, we had sufficient patients at Broadgreen Hospital to collect the numbers needed for statistical analysis within a relatively short time.

Today randomised comparison of new surgical techniques with the previous standard operation is '*de rigeur*'. It has become the backbone of evidence-based surgery. However, our randomised controlled trial to compare the results of reversed and in-situ vein grafts in the 1980s was unique. Within a year, we had included 100 patients and six months later, we were able to show that the performance of the two techniques, within this timescale at least, was identical. Although a negative finding, it was important because it removed any obligation upon vascular surgeons to perform one operation or the other. In other words, surgeons were free to select which ever procedure they were most comfortable with and which they judged to be most appropriate for each individual patient.

I presented the results of this trial at a symposium organised by Professor Roger Greenhalgh at Charing Cross Hospital in London in 1987. In the audience was an American surgeon by the name of John Bergen. He was impressed and suggested I repeat the presentation at a meeting of the American Society for Vascular Surgery (ASVS) that was due to be held in Chicago a couple of months later. As I was not a member of ASVS he offered to 'sponsor' me. Essentially this meant that he would get some of the credit for my research but I had no problem with this. I was a complete unknown, from an unknown hospital, and it was an incredibly flattering invitation. Naturally, I accepted his offer. Also, in the audience was an English surgeon by the name of Crawford Jamieson. He was Editor of the British Journal of Surgery, which was then, and still is, one of the highest-rated scientific journals for surgery worldwide. Evidently, he was impressed by what he had heard also, and invited me to submit a manuscript of my paper to him directly with a view to publication.

It was then, and maybe still is, an inviolable rule of the ASVS that presentations to its annual meeting must relate exclusively to work that is original and unpublished. I knew this but I knew also, from previous experience, that there would be a delay, before publication of my manuscript in the British Journal of Surgery of at least six months and, as the date of the ASVS meeting was less than three months away, I was not worried. So, I submitted, both an abstract to the ASVS and a manuscript to the BJS. Unfortunately, it so happened that Crawford Jamieson had been so incredibly impressed with my paper that he bypassed the normal review process and published it in the very next edition, one month later. To my great embarrassment, the presentation to the ASVS meeting was summarily cancelled and the abstract, which had already been published and widely distributed in the programme of the meeting, was struck out with the words 'WITHDRAWN: INVALID' stamped across it. I received an angrily worded letter from John Bergan. Needless to say, I did not attend the meeting in Chicago and I assumed that, as far as I was concerned, America was now a closed door. I was disappointed but not overly so, because it had never occurred to me that I might ever feature professionally in America. However, that was not to be the end of the matter. My article in the BJS was noted by Professor Frank Veith who was Chief of Vascular Surgery at Montefiore Hospital in New York and organiser of an international vascular surgical congress, held every year in Manhattan, the week before Thanksgiving. He slotted me into that year's congress at short notice and I found myself on the stage of the Grand Ballroom at the Waldorf Astoria Hotel in November addressing thousands of vascular surgeons from all corners of the globe. Frank invited me back to speak at his meeting every year for the next 25 years.

Eileen was indeed lucky. Her bypass continued to function and her leg remained intact, free from gangrene, until she died following a stroke more than two years later. The next patient on the list that day, had a harder time.

Tom McNally was not diabetic but he was a smoker. Young Tommy took his first drag at a ciggie, sometime before his 10th birthday and now, sixty years on, he was still at it. He admitted to 20-a-day but the truth was probably more like 40. A ne'er-do-well, he had been in and out of Walton jail most of his life and had never considered taking a proper job. Burglary had been his speciality but he was quite happy to turn his hand to robbery when the opportunity arose. And he was not averse to a bit of aggravation either, if necessary. He detested authority, and there was no way, he was going to give up his ciggies because some doctor had told him to. In any case, he was hopelessly addicted and would have been quite incapable of giving up even if he had wanted to.

He started to get pain in his legs in his late 40s and when inability to run became a liability in respect of his criminal activities, he complained to his GP who referred him to my predecessor at Broadgreen Hospital, Edgar Parry. Edgar was a delightful Welshman and a very experienced vascular surgeon. Initially, he carried out an operation to unblock the arteries in both groins, a sort of Dyno-Rod job. But Tommy kept smoking and within four years, he was back to square one. This time, Edgar performed a bypass with a vein graft in his left leg and six months later he carried out a similar bypass on the right. The second bypass went horribly wrong and Tommy's right leg had to be amputated below the knee a few days later. Then, when the stump failed to heal, he had another amputation above the knee. During the course of this second amputation, Tommy suffered a major heart attack and spent more than a month in the intensive care unit. Eventually, he recovered sufficiently to be discharged from hospital and he returned to his small council flat in Kirkdale in a wheel chair. The council, or as Liverpool scousers would have it the "corpy", arranged for the doors to be widened to accommodate the wheelchair and for a downstairs toilet to be installed. He supplemented his maximum disability living allowance with cash from a trade in stolen goods and he got by quite nicely – for a time.

Then, one day, he turned up at my outpatient clinic haggard, drawn and breathless with a constant hacking cough and a festering foul-smelling left foot. Slumped in his wheelchair he was incoherent and barely conscious. Whether through alcohol, painkillers, illicit drugs, lack of sleep or a combination of all these things, I could not tell. Down his front, his clothes were bespattered with cigarette burns, ash, food remnants and urine. His right trouser leg was fastened up over his thigh with safety pins and his left foot was wrapped up in a big ball of, once white now dirty grey, bandaging. Removal of the bandage, which involved a protracted process of soaking and cutting because it was firmly stuck to the tissues beneath, revealed foul putrefaction with infected, soggy gangrene affecting his first, second and third toes and a black patch of dead skin on the top of his foot.

The remainder of his foot and ankle was red and angry due to spreading infection. The odour of decay was unbearable.

After a week in hospital on intravenous antibiotics, regular dressings and morphine, he no longer looked as though he was about to die. An X-ray showed blockage of the graft and all of the main arteries in his leg. There was just one small artery visible in his lower calf. By any standards, he was a terrible candidate for surgery. He was breathless and coughing up foul green sputum, his heart was feeble and he was chronically malnourished following months of pain and not much sustenance other than alcohol. His quality of life was awful and I suspect the majority of my surgical colleagues would have opted for end-of-life care at that point rather than offering him another operation. However, the presumptuousness of making a judgement about another person's quality of life and then acting to end it never sat comfortably with me and Tommy was a case in point. There were two surgical options possible; either to attempt another bypass or to amputate the leg. I decided on the former. Tommy himself, was beyond caring, and was not interested in explanations. Resignedly, he scrawled his name illegibly on the dotted line and accepted whatever fate had in store for him.

After a few more cups of coffee, a prawn mayonnaise sandwich from the canteen and an update from the nurses on the latest hospital scandals, I was ready to go. As I entered the operating room, Doris Day was singing 'Que Sera'. In idle talk about musical preferences over the operating table one day, I declared Doris Day to be one of my favourites. It was meant to be a joke but, the next day much to everyone's amusement, a Doris Day CD appeared in the theatre and 'Que Sera Sera' became my signature tune. It helped lift the mood.

There was not a single vein remaining in Tommy's body that could be fashioned into an arterial bypass. Therefore, it was a prosthetic graft or nothing. We used one constructed from a plastic material called expanded polytetrafluoroethylene or ePTFE. It would not last as long as a vein graft but Tommy's days were numbered whatever we did and it only needed to work long enough to take the pain from his foot, for however long, he had left. Even if he had had a usable vein, we would have chosen to use a prosthetic graft, which had one important advantage over a vein graft, in that the operation was relatively quick and easy.

I had numerous patients like Tommy, who for one reason or another, had a bypass in the leg with a prosthetic, rather than a vein, graft. They worked well for a time but most were blocked within 2 years. The reason why they did not last as well as vein grafts was far from clear. Most often, the critical problem seemed to be at the junction with the natural artery at the bottom end of the graft. The lower down the leg, the smaller are the arteries. At the ankle, the average artery has a diameter of about one millimetre. Technically, I could usually make a clean join to these small arteries with very fine stitches but over time scar tissue tended to build up around the stitching to, eventually, block the artery and the graft. This did not happen, to the same extent with grafts constructed from natural veins and the challenge was to understand why.

Some possible answers to this question came from an unexpected quarter. In Australia, a vascular surgeon by the name of Justin Miller had the misfortune to develop a tremor in his hands. Consequently, stitching grafts to small arteries was problematical for him. He found, he could manage better with natural veins than with prosthetic grafts, which were stiffer and less compliant than veins, and he came up with the idea of stitching a 'cuff' of vein onto the artery first and then stitching the prosthetic graft to the cuff. It was always possible to find a small piece vein sufficient to make a cuff. In 1984, Justin Miller published a paper describing his technique, which became known as the 'Miller Cuff', and he reported a small series of patients. His results were far better than anyone had ever achieved with prosthetic grafts before.

I tried out a few of the Miller Cuffs at Broadgreen Hospital, but was not convinced that they added anything. I did not have a tremor and was reluctant to accept that making the stitching easier was likely to offer any benefit to my patients. Then, in 1985, I became Chairman of a small organisation in the UK called the Joint Vascular Research Group or JVRG. It had two aims, vascular surgical research and trout fishing. That year, I organised the meeting at Kirkby Lonsdale in the Lake District. We stayed at The Sun Inn, fished a local tarn nearby and discussed vascular surgical research over very acceptable food and wine in the evening. At this meeting, someone suggested that the Miller Cuff might be a good subject for a JVRG multi-centred randomised trial. Half the patients would get the Cuff and half would not, on a random basis, and the number of grafts remaining open over time in each group would be compared.

The results published two years later showed unequivocally that ePTFE bypasses, did indeed perform significantly better, if combined with a vein cuff and its use became our routine practice at Broadgreen Hospital. However, I remained intrigued to understand why it worked because this was still not explained. I could not accept that it was just a matter of making the operation technically easier and speculated that the cuff might have some beneficial effect on the build-up of scar tissue in the artery at the lower anastomosis. We saw X-ray evidence of this but the mechanism remained totally obscure. Fortunately, I knew someone who I thought might be able to shed some light on the matter. His name was Thien How. Thien was a lecturer in the Department of Clinical Engineering at Liverpool University. Of Chinese origin, from the Indian Ocean Island of Mauritius, he was quietly spoken, understated and a deep-thinker. His expertise was in fluid dynamics. He knew with certainty that the Miller Cuff would affect the way the blood streamed across the junction between the graft and the artery and was enthusiastic to find out how.

Thien set up some ingenious laboratory experiments to visualise the streaming of fluids across model junctions without and with cuffs. The results were unexpected. Inside the cuff, a vortex or whirlpool formed with each pulse beat. Initially, we thought that, if anything, this would be counterproductive in terms of scar formation. But then, Thien performed a second series of complex experiments and demonstrated that the vortex spinning within the cuff exerted friction on the inner wall of the artery in a way that had potential to suppress the formation of scar tissue.

The way in which blood streams across a junction is determined by the internal shape of the junction, irrespective of whether that shape is created by a vein cuff or something else. It was a small logical step to conclude that vein was not essential to the internal configuration of the cuff. The same shape could be reproduced by another material. ePTFE is a plastic polymer that can be moulded into any desired shape, including that of a cuff and we surmised that a graft with a built-in cuff would do just as well as, and possibly better than, one constructed from a piece of vein. We also reasoned that while the shape of a cuff fashioned from a piece of vein was variable, one formed from ePTFE incorporated into the end of the graft, would ensure an 'optimal' shape every time.

It was not to be the perfect solution. The results were still not as good as those of bypasses constructed entirely from the patients' own veins. But, prompted by repeated failures in desperate patients like Tom McNally, who had no useable veins left, we had evolved a concept, backed up by experimentation, that offered a significantly better chance of success than an unmodified prosthetic graft and without the time consuming and technically demanding need to construct a cuff from a piece of vein. After the best part of ten years of laboratory and clinical experimentation, we realised there might be some commercial value in a 'pre-cuffed' prosthetic arterial graft and registered a patent.

There are unavoidable legal and administrative costs associated with registering and maintaining patents, 97 per cent of which turn out to have no commercial value. We were incredibly lucky. Unknown to us, a Medical Device Company in the United States called Impra had been working with a surgeon from East Germany by the name of Schultz on a similar project. Schultz's focus was on access shunts constructed from ePTFE in the arms of patients with kidney-failure who needed regular dialysis. In contrast to bypass grafts in the legs for occlusive arterial disease the blood flow through dialysis access shunts is very rapid and this causes turbulence especially at the junctions with the arteries. Turbulence strongly promotes scarring in the arteries and therefore blockage of the shunt. Although the haemodynics are different scarring is the common pathway for the failure in both situations and Schultz had come up with a similar solution. He found that by flaring out the ends of the ePTFE shunt, he could change the shape of the junction in a way that reduced turbulence and therefore scarring. The shape of the Schultz cuff was different to ours because the haemodynamics of the two situations were different but the concepts were identical. Impra had attempted to register a US patent on behalf of Schultz but by an enormous stroke of luck, our patent application predated theirs by just one month. This was disclosed by the searches undertaken by the authorities in the US and Impra had no choice other than to accept that our intellectual property had precedence over theirs. We agreed to license our patent to them for a fee.

In 1983, all of that was still to come. Justin Miller's paper describing his cuff did not appear until 1984. So, the bypass in Tom McNally's leg did not have a cuff. Three days after operation, he had another heart attack and went into heart failure. His graft then thrombosed and the tissues in his remaining leg began to decompose rapidly. He perished the following day. The operation had served only to hasten his death.

As I came out of the operating room, Thelma put another mug of coffee on the table next to my favourite chair. It was just after 5 pm and there were still two operations to go; both amputations.

The first paper I ever published in a scientific journal was entitled 'The Fate of Elderly Amputees'. It appeared in print, in the British Journal of Surgery in 1974, when I was a surgical registrar in Manchester. Its purpose was to highlight the disastrous effect of leg amputations on patients with vascular disease, most of whom were, indeed, elderly. More than half were dead within six months and less than a quarter ever walked again with an artificial limb. At that time, amputation at mid-thigh level was standard. My first boss, Professor Michael Boyd who was himself very proficient with a fearsome amputation knife, would never countenance anything else, believing that, at a lower level, the wound would never heal. A more enlightened approach evolved with time when it was realised that patients did much better in terms of both survival and mobility afterwards, if the knee joint could be preserved.

Derek Isaacs was 42 years old. His left big toe and the adjoining second and third toes were black and shrivelled with dry gangrene. He had unmitigated pain. X-rays showed that the blood vessels in his feet and toes were blocked, although, those higher up in his leg, appeared relatively normal. He was suffering from an uncommon condition affecting his arteries called Buerger's disease.

Dr Buerger worked in New York City in the early part of the 20th century. His patients were mostly Jewish men who smoked, and he concluded that the disease he found there was unique to this population. He was partially right. Buerger's disease affects only people who smoke but is not confined to Jews or men. Stopping smoking is the cure. But, individuals subject to Buerger's disease are invariably hopelessly addicted. I had a patient once, with both legs and parts of his upper limbs amputated, who would sit in his wheelchair at the hospital entrance smoking a cigarette held between the stumps of a finger and thumb of his one remaining hand.

So, I had no illusion that Derek would give up smoking permanently. Taking his leg off, below the knee, would relieve his pain for the time being but, in all probability, he would be dead within ten years. I had not yet managed to persuade the hospital to buy me a reciprocating mechanical saw and it took me about an hour and a half to amputate his lower leg, sawing through the bones with a handsaw.

Amputations were always left to the end of the operating list, not least because infected gangrene posed a risk of cross-infection to other patients. The final patient of the day was a typical example. Annie James had diabetic gangrene in her left foot. It had started as a minor infection in a corn on the sole of her foot and now foul-smelling brown pus was seeping through a break in the skin between two black toes. It had taken no more than a few days to get to this state. Still she had no pain. In fact, she had no sensation in either foot because of her diabetes. We would investigate her circulation later. The immediate priority was to drain the pus and cut away the tissues in her foot that had been destroyed already by the rampant infection. The end result was a bizarrely bovine cleft foot in appearance, but it did the job.

As Annie was wheeled out of the operating room and I started to write the final operation note of the day, it was coming up to 7.30 pm. Thelma was still there, to hand me that last cup of coffee. Before leaving the hospital, I checked on Derek Isaacs, who was still in the recovery room next-door and then paid a quick visit to the wards. Thankfully, all was quiet so I headed for the exit and home.

A few years later, when my finances had improved a little, I bought Thelma a return air ticket to visit her brother in Australia.

Chapter 4
Riots and Other Conflicts

On a muggy evening in July 1981, a young Afro-Caribbean man named Leroy Cooper was arrested by the police on Selbourne Street in Toxteth, an area of once-grand terraced Victorian houses in inner city Liverpool. The well-to-do middle classes had deserted Toxteth long ago and it was occupied by a shifting population attracted by cheap accommodation; the unemployed, immigrants looking for a toehold in a new country, a smattering of students and destitute individuals who had fallen on hard times. Leroy Cooper's arrest attracted the attention of a crowd of on-lookers. Name-calling grew into jostling, then bricks were thrown and within minutes, there was a full-scale fracas in which three policemen were injured. What happened next was to change the face of Liverpool forever. For nine days and nine nights, Toxteth was the scene of some of the most violent riots ever witnessed in Britain. Over 450 police officers were injured, 500 people were arrested, one man died and more than 70 buildings were burnt down in pitched battles between youths, both black and white, and the police. It did not take a genius to conclude that, as Lord Scarman stated in his report subsequently, 'complex political, social and economic factors' had created a 'disposition towards violent protest'.

We had arrived in Liverpool in 1979, the year in which Margaret Thatcher first came to power. We tried hard to dismiss our negative preconceptions but initially there was little to dissuade us that the widely held prejudices about the city were not well-founded. Unemployment was at a record high and there was evidence of severe deprivation everywhere.

Many of the city centre buildings were run down and shabby. The Albert Dock – now a mecca for millions of well-heeled tourists congregating in its chic bars and restaurants – was a tumbled-down rat-infested ruin. No self-respecting citizen dared to enter. At night, the streets were dangerous and deserted. The poorer, inner-city suburbs were dirty and litter-strewn with graffiti-daubed metal security grills protecting the local convenience store and ubiquitous betting shops against robberies, that were a daily fact of life. Their famed scouse sense of humour could not conceal the dispiritedness and despair of the many decent people. Nor the pent-up frustration and anger, that was to erupt into insurrection of such violence, that even Margaret Thatcher was shaken out of her complacency.

As I write this, disaffected youths are rioting on the streets of Paris, purportedly in support of workers' rights. Policemen are being injured and property destroyed. Their violent insurrection had been planned and coordinated through social media. They wore balaclavas and ski masks to avoid recognition. Disowned by the French unions whose legitimate peaceful protests they had seized upon to provide cover for their attacks upon the police, there is no apparent justification, or indeed purpose, other than nihilistic anarchy. Initially, the Westminster establishment attempted to paint the Toxteth riots in this light. However, Toxteth was totally different. It was an insurrection born out of a genuine sense of hopelessness and frustration. The people were downtrodden and had no one to speak for them. No one cared. Their reaction was spontaneous and unplanned. Violent civil disobedience is rarely justifiable but, on this occasion, it was certainly understandable. And, it was effective. A reluctant, conservative government was provoked into investing some money on Merseyside. Margaret Thatcher must have been gnashing her teeth. The last thing she wanted, was to be seen to be indulging 'feckless' Scousers, but the national outrage at these events was such that she had no choice. Michael Heseltine was appointed Minister for Merseyside in the Cabinet and a quango, the Merseyside Development Corporation, was set up to channel new investment, bypassing the ailing labour local government.

Exclusion of the local politicians had an unfortunate, unintended consequence that, for a time, increased the suffering of the city. With their authority undermined, the traditional labour party stalwarts, in charge at the town hall, were ousted by an extreme left-wing bunch known as Militant Tendency, officially the Revolutionist Socialist League. Their chief spokesman was a character by the name of Derek Hatton. Claiming to be Trotskyists, spearheading the fight against capitalism on behalf of the proletariat, they finished the job of bankrupting the city by spending loads of money that simply did not exist and then setting an illegal, unsustainable budget. When the banks refused to provide any more cash to pay council employees, redundancy notices were handed out instead, and the city ground to a complete halt. Following this initial setback, sanity was restored with the election of a city Council with a Liberal Party majority. Militant were expelled from the Labour Party and disappeared into obscurity. Derek Hatton went on to pursue a highly successful, capitalistic and entrepreneurial career in Cyprus. Despite this early setback, the Toxteth riots had set in chain, a process of recovery that ultimately resulted in the exciting and vibrant city which is Liverpool today. The Toxteth riots had been the turning point.

We had found an Edwardian house in Crosby to the north of the city. It was occupied by a surgeon who was leaving Liverpool for richer pastures. He went on to become Professor of Surgery in Birmingham, President of the Royal College of Surgeons of Edinburgh, Chairman of the Conference of Postgraduate Deans and a Knight of the British Empire. In 1979, as plain Mr John Temple, he struck a hard bargain. But we loved the house. By any rational analysis, we could not afford it on my starting salary but it seemed a safe gamble that our initial penury would be transient, and we decided to buy it as a compensation for the less beguiling aspects of our move to Liverpool.

The house was situated on a quiet leafy road just off the main road north to Southport. On the other side of the main road there was a housing estate known locally as 'Colditz'. It earned this sobriquet for good reason. It was bleak. Shortly after we arrived, a man was thrown to his death from the top of one of the tower blocks for reasons that we never fully ascertained but assumed to be related to the gang wars, which were rife. The local state primary school was populated by "scallies" from Colditz. They were probably great kids but it seemed unlikely that scholastic learning would feature highly amongst their interests. Carole made it clear from the very start, that our boys were not going to go to that school for their education. Merchant Taylors was the preeminent school in north Liverpool and the main reason why we chose to live there. However, there was a waiting list and we could not get our boys in to start with. Accordingly, we enrolled them into a private primary school in Formby, a couple of miles away.

Most people would reasonably assume that promotion to a consultant post in surgery would bring immediate financial rewards. My reward was the opposite, a catastrophic cut in salary. While the intra-aortic balloon pump programme at Charing Cross Hospital had boosted my overtime payments as a senior registrar to a maximum, Liverpool Health Authority contrived to start me on the lowest possible consultant salary. They did have a choice. To be fair their lack of generosity was probably not so much a reflection of their opinion of my worth as pressure upon them to cut their budget. There was a new Conservative government and times were hard. They even refused to pay the removal expenses to which we were entitled. I was not too worried because I had counted upon earning sufficient additional income from private practice to cover our costs. I rented a room in Rodney Street, the Harley Street of Liverpool, straight away and waited for the private patients to roll in. Eighteen months passed, before the very first one knocked on my door. An anaesthetic colleague at the hospital, seeing my plight, took pity on me and persuaded his GP wife to refer a patient to me with a hernia. Another five years passed before I was generating sufficient income from it to cover the costs of private practice. A frightening consequence of the resulting disparity between income and expenditure was, that for several months, our mortgage repayments on the house actually exceeded my net salary. An untenable situation, however you looked at it. While we struggled to pay for the basics, the house remained uncarpeted and unfurnished apart from one room, the sitting room. This had a nice new carpet and curtains, courtesy of my parents, but we never went in it for fear of messing it up and the door remained firmly closed. Carole's father, who was not a rich man by any means, offered to pay the school fees for the boys from his life savings. We accepted his offer with gratitude and reluctance in equal measure.

Fortunately, we were rescued from our financial plight, by a totally unanticipated change in policy towards private medical practice initiated by the new conservative government. When I started at Broadgreen Hospital, I was obliged to accept a considerably reduced 'part-time' salary for the privilege of engaging in private practice. As it turned out, this was a seriously bad move. Not only, did I not have any private patients, but given the vast unmet demand for vascular surgery in the NHS in Liverpool, I found myself putting in many more hours of work than those of my consultant colleagues who had opted for full-time salaries. Under the Conservatives 'New Deal', which was designed to ease the legacy of unrest fomented by the attack on private practice by the previous Labour health minister, a belligerent left-wing battle axe called Barbara Castle, 'full-time' consultants would be permitted to earn additional income from private practice up to ten per cent of their salary without forfeit. I immediately applied to convert to a full-time contract. This, together with an increase in all doctors' pay and an incremental increase due to me at the end of the first year, enabled us to get by. But it was another five years before the rest of the house was carpeted.

While all of this was going on, I was trying to get myself established professionally. It was hard going. I suppose, as an outsider, I should not have expected more but, with few notable exceptions, the level of enthusiasm that greeted my arrival was muted, to put it politely.

Broadgreen hospital began its existence as a typical Victorian TB sanatorium, with a row of single-storey pavilions connected by one long corridor. Then, during the Second World War, it was expanded by construction of another row of single-storey pavilions connected by a parallel corridor. These wartime buildings were thrown up hurriedly to accommodate wounded Canadian soldiers and had never been intended to last beyond the duration of the war. The walls were just one brick thick and had no cavity for insulation. Without any buttressing, they had bowed alarmingly and had to be shored up with external timbers. Central heating had been installed but, when I arrived, there was an old iron stove still standing in a corner of one of the wards.

The only new building on the site was the Cardiothoracic Centre (CTC). Its presence was a legacy of the origins of the hospital as an asylum for patients with TB, which had been a common early indication for operations on the chest. Later, when heart-lung machines had been invented, chest surgery evolved to include open-heart operations. The heart and the blood vessels are parts of the same cardiovascular system and subject to similar pathologies occurring in the same population of patients. Moreover, the surgical techniques and the facilities required have much in common. For this reason, to me at least, it made clinical and economic sense that cardiac and vascular surgery should be combined into a single cardiovascular speciality. This is an arrangement that works well in many of the larger and most successful hospitals in Europe and the United States, but not the UK. Given that I had had training and experience in cardiac as well as vascular surgery at Charing Cross Hospital, it occurred to me that I was in a good position to forge a relationship along these lines at Broadgreen Hospital with the added benefit of accessing the superior facilities of the CTC. So, I made an approach to the Head of the CTC, an irascible Irish man by the name of Ben Meade. He wasn't remotely interested and, very obviously irritated that I should suggest anything so ridiculous, he hardly gave me the time of day. My frustration was heightened by the fact that there seemed to be no limit to the money Liverpool Health Authority was prepared to spend on cardiac surgery while I was struggling to secure funding for even the most basic equipment for vascular surgery and, on top of that, I was desperately overworked. In my desperation I applied for a job at the North Shore Hospital in Sydney, Australia but they didn't want me either.

The one thing there was no shortage of at Broadgreen Hospital was vascular patients. It had been an inauspicious start and there were many more times, when I had thought to escape, but steadily I became immersed in a challenging and immensely rewarding routine of work and my discontentment waned. As the years passed Liverpool truly became 'home' for me and my family, and we grew to be immensely proud to be identified with that city and its people.

Then, as now, in order to advance your speciality within the NHS, you have to fight for your corner. This has the unfortunate tendency to reward those who shout the loudest, irrespective of the merits of their case. Given that the facilities for vascular surgery at Broadgreen Hospital were so rudimentary, I had no choice but to engage with the system and its politics. Initially, progress was painfully slow but in 1988, I was appointed Medical Director of the Hospital. This role carried a certain amount of influence in respect of resource allocation but was a double-edged sword because I could hardly be seen to be promoting vascular surgical priorities over those of other specialities without incurring accusations of corrupt self-interest. Despite my best efforts in this regard, my tenure as Medical Director ended in 1992 in bitter conflict and fierce recriminations.

In 1988, the Thatcher government decided to impose an 'internal market' within the NHS with a split between purchasers and providers. The rationale was to create greater efficiency through competition. So, The Royal and Broadgreen began competing with each other for 'business'. Soon it became clear that there was insufficient money available for both of them to continue to provide a complete range of acute services and the fate of the Accident and Emergency Department at Broadgreen Hospital became central to the debate that ensued. Compared to that at the Royal in the city centre, the Broadgreen A&E Department was small but its existence demanded the support of a full range of acute specialities. It was clear to me that this was going to be unsustainable. Accordingly I came up with a proposal for Broadgreen to relinquish its A&E Department in order to focus on a future as a 'centre of excellence' for elective medicine and surgery. It was not a popular plan with a number of my consultant colleagues!

At the same time, I was engaged in a bitter internal struggle within my own vascular surgery unit. In the 60s and 70s, a radiologist in Seattle, on the west coast of the USA, called Charles Dotter had been 'Dyno-Rod-ing' blocked arteries with metal dilators. The main advantage of this was that it was done under X-ray guidance without major surgery. For a long time, nobody took him seriously. In fact, many considered him to be seriously 'unhinged' and he came known in vascular surgery circles as 'Mad Charlie' Dotter. But then, in the late-70s, a German radiologist called Andreas Gruentzig invented a device that gave credence to the concept of treating blocked arteries without major surgery. Gruentzig's invention was a balloon that could be expanded to a predetermined size and shape under high pressure on the end of a long thin catheter. With the requisite skill the balloon could be advanced through the vascular system under X-ray guidance to any artery in the body and then pressurised to open up a blockage or narrowing. Minimally invasive treatment of vascular disease that avoided the dangers of major surgery had become a real possibility. In 1977, Andreas Gruentzig performed the first coronary artery balloon angioplasty procedure on a patient in Zurich with ischaemic heart disease. This was the first of many millions of such procedures that soon became established as standard practice throughout the world.

At Broadgreen Hospital, I was working with a radiologist called Derek Gould. He did the X-rays, I did the surgery. We were a good team - until I started to take an interest in Gruentzig's 'balloon angioplasty' methods. What ensued was a struggle that was replicated in hospitals all around the Country and indeed, the world; a battle between surgeons and radiologists as to who should perform balloon angioplasty. It is a big money-spinner in private medical practice and in places where private care dominates, such as America, competition was inevitable. Within the socialised British healthcare system and especially in Liverpool, where money was never a consideration, it was entirely counterproductive. Nevertheless, Derek took a particularly hard-line stance, with bitter consequences. In his role as senior radiologist he was responsible for radiation-safety in the hospital, and he had no hesitation in denying me access to all X-ray imaging equipment and the radiographers who operated it. This was despite the fact that I had a radiation safety certificate. He effectively prevented me, personally, from undertaking balloon angioplasty treatments in the NHS at that time. On the other hand Derek did not have direct access to patients and he could only treat those I referred to him. So, little progress was made.

Given my conflict with Derek over this matter, it was no surprise to find him on the opposing side in respect of the Broadgreen A&E department issue. The forum for debate of hospital policies was the Medical Board, which was composed of the clinical leads for each speciality and senior managers. As Medical Director I chaired the meetings. In 1992, the internal market 'crunch' arrived and we had to make a decision about Broadgreen Hospital's 'pitch' in the competition for resources with the Royal. I knew that my proposal to cede A&E services would be met with hostility and was prepared for some robust debate. I had prepared my arguments but, when it came up on the agenda of the Medical Board, there was no debate. Raising a point of order, Derek accused me of misconduct in office and demanded a vote of no-confidence in me as Medical Director. He claimed, without any foundation, that I had misappropriated hospital funds in favour of vascular surgery. I looked around for support but there was none and had no choice other than to accede to his demand. I was comprehensively defeated on a show of hands. It had been well worked 'hatchet job' by the 'Save Broadgreen A&E' brigade.

Though that incident was uncomfortable and unpleasant, it had no lasting consequences for me or for the hospital. Later, in that same year of 1992, a decision was made by Liverpool Health Authority to rationalise vascular services into a single unit based at the Royal and I was relocated. It was also decided that the Accident and Emergency Department at Broadgreen Hospital would be closed and that the Broadgreen site would be developed as a centre for elective surgery.

The rationalisation of services that followed in Liverpool, and other big cities, was seen by 'free-market' politicians of the day as proof of the benefit of 'supermarket' style competition between healthcare providers. However, the conversion of NHS services into a commodities to be traded, was never in the interests of patients. It was simply a means of cutting costs under the guise of improving healthcare efficiency. By 1997, when the conservatives finally lost power again after 18 years in government, the NHS was in a state of disrepair and despair. Hospitals were falling apart, more than a million patients were on waiting lists, there were far too few staff, and standards of care across the Country were in decline. The very survival of the NHS was in question and it took an enormous cash injection by the Blair government to turn it around.

By the late 1980s, the vascular surgical workload at Broadgreen Hospital had become insupportable for a 'single-handed' consultant. Out-of-hours emergencies were depriving me of sleep and of my family at weekends. Vascular services in North Wales, Cheshire and most of West Lancashire were still either non-existent or rudimentary, and patients with ruptured aortic aneurysms from this wide geographical area were still being 'blue-lighted' into Liverpool. The vascular surgeon at the Royal, was similarly 'single-handed' and simply not coping. So, we agreed a system by which emergencies at night and at weekends, would be diverted to one hospital or the other, according to an agreed rota. Although this was an improvement we were still being overwhelmed with non-urgent referrals at Broadgreen Hospital. Patients were waiting more than two years for a first appointment and then, another two years after that for X-rays and surgery. There was considerably less pressure on the service at the Royal, but my suggestion to access resources there for Broadgreen patients was flatly refused. Apparently as a district general hospital consultant I did not merit the privilege of access to the teaching hospital. My increasingly desperate requests for a second vascular consultant at Broadgreen also fell on deaf ears. Then help arrived from an unexpected quarter.

The regional kidney transplantation unit at the Royal, was led by a surgeon, by the name of Robert Sells. A flamboyant, theatrical character with a penchant for rakish clothes, classical music and self-promotion. In his spare time he conducted an orchestra Crosby, where he lived, with the flourish and gusto of a maestro. I have no idea whether he was any good or not. Robert decided he was overworked and needed help. Being far better connected than I was, he had the clout to get his way. However, Robert revelled in his role as the Liverpool transplant surgeon and did not want anyone to challenge his vaunted status. Accordingly, he proposed to appoint a part-time transplant surgeon and suggested that whoever was appointed might lend a hand to vascular surgery with the remainder of his time. The vascular surgeon at the Royal, who suffered even greater insecurity than Robert, was not interested, so I was approached at Broadgreen. I was reluctant to agree to the proposal at first because I really needed another fully trained and committed whole-time vascular surgeon and the chances of getting one would be scuppered for the foreseeable future. However, 'a bird in the hand …'. In this case the bird's name was Ali Bakran. Well-trained in kidney transplantation, he had scant experience in vascular surgery and required a lot of support initially but, in time, he made a valuable, and much needed, contribution to the vascular workload at Broadgreen. Ironically, it was not long before Robert fell out with him, and tried to get rid of him. He did not succeed but a bitter war between them endured unceasingly until Robert finally retired 20 or more years later.

The clinical trials and experimental tweaks we came up with, in the early years at Broadgreen Hospital, were not revolutionary by any means. On the contrary, they were extremely modest. They did, however, attract some interest in the outside world and in the mid-1980s, we started to receive visits from vascular surgeons from neighbouring hospitals, then from other parts of the UK and then from Europe and Scandinavia. Impra, the American Company that manufactured and distributed our pre-cuffed arterial grafts under the names, Distaflo and Dynaflo, had a commercial interest in promoting me as their salesman and they sponsored regular vascular surgery workshops on our unit at Broadgreen. These events consisted of a day in the operating room, followed by dinner in the evening at a restaurant or at the Liverpool Racquet Club, where I was a member. Impra took care of all travel and accommodation costs of the guests and this ensured a steady stream of participants, some of whom were actually interested in what we were doing. In this way, I got to know, and be known by people outside the narrow confines of little Broadgreen Hospital in the lesser-known suburbs of Liverpool. However, I was hardly a major league player and was more than surprised to receive, in 1988, an invitation to join the Council of the Vascular Surgical Society of Great Britain and Ireland.

Chapter 5
Jack Jones

One Thursday morning, I was called into the Medical Director's office at the Royal. Having transferred from Broadgreen Hospital in 1992, I had been there for two years. Austin Carty was an affable Irish radiologist originally from Cork. Being a colourful character, with flamboyant ginger beard, colourful bow ties and tweed suits, he was highly sociable and a well-known medical personality about town. I liked him and had thought he made a good Medical Director. But, on that Thursday morning, I formed a rather different opinion. In retrospect, he was merely the messenger but it seemed to me that he discharged his duty with unnecessary vigour. Basically, he offered me a choice between 'towing the line' or looking for a new job!

A few weeks earlier, at his home on the Wirral, Jack Jones had had a 'funny turn'. Jack smoked 'a bit' but considered himself to be in good shape and, having just retired from work as a financial advisor at the age of 65, he was looking forward to spending more time on the golf course. He and his wife, Frances, had just sat down for dinner at home. Nothing special; omelette and chips at the kitchen table while watching the BBC 6 o'clock news. His mind was on the news when, suddenly, his knife clattered onto the tiled floor.

Cursing his clumsiness under his breath, he bent to pick it up, but couldn't.

His fingers refused to close on the handle. Frances noticed him fumbling. 'What's up Jack?" she asked.

"Dunno," he replied, "Cramp or something." Frances picked up the knife and placed it on the plate for him while he sat back again bending and straightening the fingers with his other hand. He seemed perplexed and Frances felt a surge of anxiety. Something strange was happening. He looked OK but she could see that his fingers were still not moving and it did not seem to her like typical cramp. In any case, Jack did not get cramp, so why now? She picked up the phone, not sure whether to call their daughter, who worked as a nurse in Manchester, 30 miles away, or the doctor. In the end, she did neither because she heard Jack say, "Just a second. I think it's coming back," and she put the 'phone down again. A couple of minutes later, Jack's hand was back to normal. It was as if nothing had happened. He flexed his fingers a few times, then shrugged his shoulders and went back to eating his omelette and chips.

Frances said nothing for the moment but remained unsettled by what had happened and she called her daughter later. She was adamant, "Call the GP, first thing in the morning. It may well have been nothing but it's just not worth taking the chance. Dad could have had a small stroke."

The daughter's intuition was correct. Jack had had a stroke; a 'mini-stroke'. Doctors call it a 'Transient Cerebral Ischaemic Attack' or TIA. Although fleeting and seemingly trivial, it forewarned of something altogether more calamitous; a major stroke that could leave him paralysed and unable to speak, or dead. The GP contacted Arrow Park, the local hospital on the Wirral, for an urgent appointment and two days later, Jack was seen by Dr Peter Humphrey. Peter was a consultant at the Regional Centre for Neurology and Neurosurgery, based at Walton Hospital to the northeast of Liverpool city centre. He conducted regular outreach clinics at other hospitals, including Arrow Park. We had been working together for some time on patients like Jack Jones.

Ministrokes result from narrowing of the carotid arteries in the neck. They are the largest arteries supplying blood to the brain. When they block slowly due to disease the problem is not that blood flow to the brain is reduced. There is a rich inter-connected network of arteries supplying the brain and there is plenty of spare capacity if one, two or even three vessels become narrowed or blocked. This is nature's insurance policy to protect the body's most vital organ. Strokes occur, under these circumstances, because fatty material which accumulates in the artery, to cause the blockage, is loose and bits break off and are carried into the brain. A tiny fragment causes a ministroke and a big one, a major stroke. Frequently, ministrokes precede and forewarn of impending disaster. However, provided a ministroke is recognised for what it is the risk of following a major stroke can be averted by a timely operation to remove the source of narrowing. Diagnosis and rapid referral is critical and does not always happen because the symptoms of a ministroke can appear quite trivial. Luckily for Jack his daughter was switched on to the risks he faced.

Operative intervention for ministrokes is now established treatment but in the 1980s it was far from clear that surgery on carotid arteries could be undertaken safely or that strokes could be prevented. Operating upon arteries supplying the brain has obvious risks and the issue initially was whether operating would cause more strokes than it prevented. In the second half of the decade, a European-wide, multicentred trial took place in an attempt to answer this question. Peter Humphrey and I joined forces in Liverpool to recruit patients and at the end of the trial, we had contributed data on more patients than any other participating centre. The large number of patients from Merseyside, reflected partly, the high prevalence of the problem in our part of the world but also our shared eagerness to resolve the practicalities of how to manage the many patients who presented to us with ministrokes. The results of this clinical trial, first published in 1991, showed that in patients with severely narrowed carotid arteries, surgery reduced the risk of major stroke and death eight-fold. What was also clear from the results of this trial was that the risk of a major stroke was highest in the days immediately following a TIA. Therefore, surgical treatment had to be undertaken urgently in order 'not to miss the boat'.

So, in 1992, Peter Humphrey and I had an agreed protocol for treatment of patients like Jack Jones. He identified and referred patients who were most at risk and I performed the surgery on the very next operating list. Sometimes, this meant that less urgent operations had to be postponed to accommodate them.

The key to making the surgery safe is effective protection of the brain. Other than the risk of TIA, slow blockage of a carotid artery due to progressive disease is very well tolerated for the reason explained previously. Sudden occlusion due to bungled surgery is altogether another matter.

The first ever-successful operation on a carotid artery was carried out at St. Mary's Hospital in London in 1954 by an Englishman called Felix Eastcott. It was a very daring thing to do because accepted wisdom at the time was that a stroke was almost inevitable. Eastcott was lucky, or rather the patient was, because despite doing nothing to protect the blood supply to the brain during clamping of the artery, he got away with it that one time. However, subsequent experience over the next 30 years or so was far from positive. Despite the introduction of various ingenious techniques designed to reduce the risks, stroke and death rates associated with operations on the carotid arteries remained prohibitively high. My first experiences were in Manchester in the 1970s working for a well-known and highly regarded vascular surgeon called David

Charlesworth. He immersed patients in baths of iced water to reduce their body temperature, and therefore that of the brain, to around 30°C. It was believed that at this temperature, the brain could be safely deprived of a blood supply for about seven minutes. He then had to work quickly against the clock to complete the operation within this time. It is unfortunately the case that, as far as delicate surgery is concerned, haste is not conducive to safety. Also, if you overdo the cooling by a couple of degrees the heart has a tendency to stop. Dreadful results soon led to this technique being abandoned.

The breakthrough came eventually with the development of shunts. These are tubes of plastic that are inserted into the artery above and below the operation site to maintain the flow of blood to the brain throughout the procedure.

When the tests on Jack Jones confirmed he was a high-risk candidate for a major stroke, Peter Humphrey called me and I arranged for him to be admitted to the Royal that same evening for operation, the next day. The list was full, so Jack took the place of a lady who was to have surgery for varicose veins.

It was this incident that led to my confrontation with the Medical Director.

Jack was apprehensive on arrival to the ward. Everything was happening a bit fast, which reinforced in him the notion that he was in serious trouble. The prospect of any sort of surgery is frightening and one involving the brain doubly so. Frances was trying, unconvincingly, to appear calm. I reiterated what they had been told already by Peter Humphrey; that the surgery carried very little risk and was many times safer than doing nothing under his circumstances.

By 8.30, the next morning, he was anaesthetised and on the operating table with his head settled into a foam rubber ring to extend his neck. He was covered with green sterile towels, apart from a window over the carotid artery on the left side of his neck, which was exposed beneath a clear plastic adhesive. The scalpel sliced cleanly through the skin along the edge of the muscle overlying the carotid artery beneath the jaw and, as blood oozed up along the line of the incision, bleeding points were sealed with an electric cautery. The carotid artery is a large pulsating vessel that passes vertically out of the chest into the neck. Just behind the angle of the jaw, it splits into two. The front part splits again into multiple other branches to supply the face, while the part at the back continues to run up vertically through a hole in the base of the skull, into the brain as a single branch. For complex and incompletely understood reasons, the artery is vulnerable to disease where it divides in the neck and it is here, that fatty material accumulates, waiting to be dislodged. I could feel a hard lump at this point in Jack's artery. It had to be handled with great care for fear of precipitating the stroke we were trying to prevent

Jeff, the anaesthetist, administered heparin to prevent the blood from clotting and after waiting a couple of minutes for it to circulate, I clamped off the main carotid artery and its two branches. It took another couple of minutes to insert the shunt. One end went into the main artery and the other into the branch supplying the brain. The other branch was simply clamped because the face can survive for a long time without a blood supply. I, then, made an incision in the artery to expose and remove the disease that was narrowing it. That done, we closed the artery with a patch of Dacron fabric to ensure that no narrowing remained and finally removed the shunt. By 10 o'clock, Jack was waking up in 'recovery' and half an hour later, we were able to confirm that he could speak and that all parts of his body were moving normally his right hand included. Next morning, he was in great form and was ready to go home as I knocked on the Medical Director's door and waited to be invited to enter.

It was early 1991, when the conservative government introduced a Patients' Charter, which outlined the rights of patients and the quality of service they should expect to receive. This Charter included specific targets for waiting times for hospital treatment. The problem was that there was not then, nor has there ever been, sufficient capacity in the NHS to meet all the demands placed upon it. Left to doctors, resources are rationed according to medical priorities, meaning that those with the greatest need are treated first. For the first time in its history, but certainly not the last, this government decided to over-ride the advice of doctors and set targets which had more to do with political expediency than medical priority. One of the first of these targets was a maximum waiting time for non-urgent surgery of two years. In the absence of any plan to facilitate realisation of this target, for example by increasing capacity, adverse consequences were inevitable. Patients with urgent needs, like Jack Jones, were in the firing line. At the Royal the waiting time for varicose vein surgery was well over two years.

After the briefest of pleasantries, Austin Carty informed me that my decision to give priority to Jack over that of a patient with varicose veins was not consistent with government directives and therefore, unacceptable. I countered that, I found it a lot less acceptable that my patient should be placed at increased risk of major stroke and death for the sake of meeting a government target for non-urgent surgery. He then told me in no uncertain terms, that if I was not prepared to comply with the policy, I would have to apply for a job elsewhere. I was incredulous and thought he must be joking. But, he quickly disabused me of that notion. Stunned and infuriated, I turned and left. It was a brief conversation!

Peter Humphrey was similarly dismayed at this turn of events. The statistical evidence was clear; delayed surgery following TIA would result in more avoidable strokes, and death. Scheduled operating lists were planned two to three weeks in advance for administrative reasons. Patients had to be contacted and they needed time to make personal arrangements for their admission. We thought about leaving one or two slots free to accommodate carotid and other urgent operations when planning the lists in the hopes the Medical Director would not notice that the waiting times for non-urgent vascular surgery were getting even longer as a consequence. We also considered re-classifying carotid surgery from 'urgent' to 'emergency' and undertaking the operations out-of-hours at night and at weekends. This might have been allowed but I feared that complication rates would increase if we operated on these patients in the middle of the night with an inexperienced 'on-call' team. We needed another plan and Peter Humphrey came up with the idea of undertaking the operations at Walton Hospital rather than at The Royal. This seemed like a possible solution but there was no one at Walton Hospital with either the experience or the inclination to operate upon carotid arteries. If this was going to happen, I would have to go to Walton Hospital to operate there myself. There was a problem with this because I had a full-time contract with the Royal and there was no chance of being released to work elsewhere. We decided to give it a try 'unofficially' and Peter secured operating rights for me at Walton without the Royal knowing. Unfortunately this surreptitious arrangement did not work out well in practice for the obvious and predictable reason that I had no skilled back-up and could not be in two places at the same time. We persisted with it for a few months by which time the initial hullaballoo about waiting targets at The Royal had died down and we simply reverted to doing exactly what we had been doing before.

The senior managers at the Royal, Austin Carty included, knew nothing about any of this. I presumed they had noted a decline in the number of last-minute cancellations of non-urgent varicose veins operations and had moved on to worry about other things. In any case nobody said anything. Austin Carty either forgot our confrontation or decided to let bygones be bygones because he reverted to being the affable Irish dandy I had known before and normal social interactions between us were resumed.

This was not the first time, nor the last, that I found myself directly at odds with government policy for the NHS. It was futile to object and I was not alone in seeking ways to compensate for or, as in this case, to circumvent, the damaging consequences for individual patients.

Following publication of the report on the European Trial and a similar one from America, which also showed unequivocal benefit from surgery, carotid endarterectomy became the most common operation to be performed by vascular surgeons everywhere. At the Royal we were operating upon a hundred plus patients a year and, despite our best efforts, one or two would suffer a procedure-related major stroke or death. Although this rate of serious complications was well within acceptable limits to ensure considerable benefit for the programme overall each and every adverse event was a cause of great consternation.

One lady in particular still remains imprinted on my memory. In her 70s, slim, elegant and charming, she had had several TIAs within a short period. As usual, after excising the disease, I closed the artery with a patch. At the time, I favoured a patch constructed from a vein harvested locally from the neck. Intuitively, it seemed to me that this would be better than the alternative constructed from Dacron fabric. I was aware of reports of vein patches giving way, but had arrogantly dismissed them as technical errors with the stitching; in other words poor surgery. Nothing like that had ever happened to any of my patients. This lady's operation had been straightforward and she was already wide-awake and in good spirits by the time I left the hospital to go home that evening. When I returned the next morning, she was dead.

The ward sister told me what had happened. She had been in a single room rather than the open ward. The nurse looking after her had been going into the room at regular intervals to check her pulse, blood pressure and inspect the wound. She was alone the rest of the time but had a call-button to call the nurse if she needed anything. All was well until just before 2.30 am when the nurse heard an unusual noise. The nurse-call button had not been pressed but she decided to check that everything was OK. On opening the door, she was met with a horrific scene. Blood spurting from the poor lady's neck was splattering on the ceiling and on the walls. A large puddle of blood on the bed was over-flowing onto the floor. The nurse hit the emergency button and screamed for help as she climbed on the bed to press on the neck to try to stop the bleeding. By the time the cardiac arrest team arrived, it was too late. The distraught nurse ended up soaked from head to toe in blood. She received post-traumatic counselling but remained off work for three months and I wonder, if she ever really fully recovered from the experience.

I had to know what happened and attended the post-mortem examination to find out. To my consternation, the vein patch had ruptured. The stitching was intact but there was a large rent in the centre. Needless to say, I never again used a vein patch to repair a carotid artery. I learned also, never to be dismissive of other surgeons' experiences no matter how improbable they may seem.

Chapter 6
Europe

High in the Italian Alps, under the shadow of Mont Blanc, the tiny alpine village of Saint Vincent nestles on an elevated plateau beneath the jagged pinnacle of The Matterhorn. For centuries, the ancient stone buildings of this village have sheltered rugged mountain farmers and their families, snuggled together around wood-burning stoves under deep winter snow, while their livestock inhabit the barn beneath. In spring time, man and beast emerge to revel in the sparkling beauty and clear mountain air of lush alpine meadows. Contented cows, with clanging bells dangling from leather straps around their necks, produce rich creamy milk from which pungent cheeses are made, according to ancient tradition, to be sold in Aosta town market in the valley below. Vestiges of this way of life, regulated as it is by nature and the seasons, still remain, but the pastoral idyll has been brutally assailed of late by an altogether different sort of culture. An incongruous modern concrete and glass monstrosity has materialised at the edge of the village. It does not accommodate skiers or alpine walkers as might be imagined, but city types with altogether less wholesome interests. Alongside a hotel, and connected to it by a short corridor, is a garish casino and nightclub.

The existence of this vulgar establishment in a previously untouched, remote alpine village is owed to a decision by the semi-autonomous local government of the Aosta Region to supplement its finances with the proceeds of gambling; a shrewd move given that gambling was illegal in the rest of Italy at the time. Gambling laws were liberalised in Italy in 2006 but in the 1980s and 90s, the casino at Saint Vincent was the only legitimate gaming establishment for many miles around. It was extremely well patronised.

The Casino had an outer area in which small-time punters, typically plump Italian ladies with cigarettes dangling from the corner of their mouths or young men with 'playboy' aspirations but modest means, worked the slot machines or chanced their hand at the roulette wheel. Under bright lights, whoops of joy and groans of despair mingled with the noisy clatter of the machines.

The serious business took place in private. Large, surly men in dark suits and dark glasses guarded the entrance to an inner 'sanctum sanctorum' in a scene, uncomfortably reminiscent of gangster soldiers guarding a 1930s prohibition-era speakeasy in Chicago. Within, the ambiance was sombre, hushed and discrete. Gentle clinking of high-value chips merged with muffled conversations as large sums of money changed hands over subtly illuminated green baize. I entered this den of iniquity quite often in the '90s as an official representative of my Country.

This task was delegated to me by The Vascular Surgical Society of GB and Ireland, which is the organisation for the vascular speciality in the British Isles and the Republic of Ireland. The word 'Surgical' was dropped from the title in 2003 in order to encourage non-surgical vascular specialists, such as interventional radiologists, to join and today, it numbers more than 800 in its membership. When first founded in 1966, there were just 26 members. The founders were general surgeons with a common interest in the new and exciting business of operating upon blood vessels. Michael Boyd, professor of surgery in Manchester at that time, and my first boss after qualification, was not a founder. In fact, he never joined The Society. With his idiosyncratic approach to vascular surgery and, indeed, to life in general, he saw no need for it and, what's more, had little admiration or respect for those who did. His views were well known: 'Operations to repair blood vessels were misguided and dangerous'. Presumably, the enthusiasts who thought otherwise were relieved that he stayed away!

By the time of my appointment as a consultant, in 1979, membership of the Vascular Surgical Society was indispensable to anyone wishing to pursue an interest in the speciality and I duly joined up. Nine years later, I was agreeably surprised to be invited to join the Council and, a year later, even more surprised to find myself elected Honorary Secretary and Treasurer. This was a big deal. With a tenure of four years, I had responsibility for the day-to-day business of The Society with some influence over its policies as determined by the Council and I was its spokesman on matters pertaining to vascular surgery nationally and occasionally internationally.

The late 1980s and early 1990s was a time of significant socio-political change in Europe where there was a drive to make the European Union project and its principle of free-movement, a reality. To enable doctors and, other professionals, to work in any country of the European Union irrespective of the member-state in which they qualified, there clearly had to be some agreed standards of training and competence to which all countries would have to conform. The process for achieving this was euphemistically called 'harmonisation' and the body with responsibility for harmonising medical practice across the European Union was called the Union Européenne Des Médecins Spécialistes or UEMS. There was a 'Section' or harmonisation committee for each speciality with a representative from each European Union member state. The relatively nascent speciality of vascular surgery was disadvantaged in this process because it had not yet been recognised as a speciality by the majority of European Union member states and this was a prerequisite for formation of a Speciality Section. In countries, like the UK, where it was not a recognised speciality, it was considered to be a part of general surgery and it was dealt with by the Section of General Surgery within the UEMS. This was a highly unsatisfactory arrangement given that most national representatives on the Section of General Surgery were breast or bowel surgeons who knew next to nothing about blood vessels. Vascular surgeons from countries where they were recognised as independent specialists were outraged and refused to cooperate. Italy was one such.

In the semi-autonomous mountainous region of Aosta, an enterprising young vascular surgeon by the name of Domenico Palombo managed to secure from his equally enterprising local government, a sum of money in support of a project with the declared aim of promoting vascular surgery as a bona fide surgical speciality within the UEMS. Representative organisations for vascular surgery in each European Union Country were invited to appoint delegates to attend meetings that took place in the Casino Hotel in the little alpine village of Saint Vincent. As secretary of the Vascular Society, I was delegated to represent the UK. The Republic of Ireland sent its own representative.

The assemblage became known as 'The Aosta Group'. Working sessions were chaired by a senior surgeon from Bologna called Massimo D'Addato. Domenico Palombo was considered too junior for this role in the highly hierarchical Italian system. Massimo D'Addato was one of a small band of 'patrician' surgeons who exercised tight control over the vascular domain in Italy and were treated with the diffidence and respect accorded to a mafia boss. Proceedings were conducted in assorted aberrations of the English language and, as a native English speaker, it was decided that I should have the job of scrivener.

As I set about the task of deciphering confused, invariably tendentious debates, a certain amount of interpretation was necessary in order to record what individuals meant to say, which was not always what they actually said. I had learned long ago that composing the minutes of meetings, conferred upon the composer considerable influence over the inferences that could be drawn from the discussions. It was a role I was content to accept. Having first agreed statutes and procedures, we set about defining the content and boundaries of the vascular speciality, followed by discussion of standards of training to be expected of someone wishing to be recognised as a vascular specialist in Europe.

After a day in the conference room, we would adjourn in the evening for sumptuous Italian food and wine in the nightclub, where we were entertained by magicians and dancing girls. This was followed by a flutter in the casino for those with the inclination.

Back in Brussels, the Section of General Surgery was preparing a concession in response to pressure from The Aosta Group and others. Rules were rules and could not be ignored but, in 1991, a decision was made to establish a Subsection of Vascular Surgery, which would be answerable to the Section of General Surgery. It was a token gesture that conferred no substantive autonomy but the patriarchs of the Section of General Surgery hoped that it might pacify the growing dissatisfaction of vascular surgeons. Many in countries like Italy, France, Spain and Greece, where vascular surgery was a recognised speciality, found the 'Subsection' label demeaning and, for them, it had the opposite effect.

Nevertheless, the plan went ahead and it fell to me again to represent vascular surgeons in the UK. At the first meeting, it had to be decided who would chair the meetings. There was not a great deal of competition for the role given the reservations surrounding the project. The French, for example, had declined any involvement, but my name was put forward and I was duly voted in. The elderly gentlemen of the Section of General Surgery had intended the Subsection to be no more than a talking shop. Any influence it might have could be exerted only through them, which left them completely in control. However, there were changes in the air, which they had not anticipated. In 1991, frustrated at the lack of progress towards harmonisation of medical practice, the powers-that-be at the centre of the UEMS decided to launch a new initiative, which happened to coincide with the formation of the Vascular Surgery Subsection. A new tier of harmonisation committees was to be established with the designation of 'Speciality Boards'. They would have enhanced power over the Sections, most importantly including that of setting examinations and awarding certificates of competence. There was nothing in the rules to prevent us setting up European Board of Vascular Surgery which we duly did with a minimum of delay. It was a significant step towards full recognition of vascular surgery as a speciality in the EU that we in the Aosta Group had been campaigning for. The Board of Vascular Surgery was one of the first to be officially inaugurated by the UEMS. The launch took place in 1994 at a meeting in Edinburgh. I was again elected chairman, this time with the ludicrously inflated title of 'President' as is the custom in continental Europe. My colleague, and friend, from Eindhoven in Holland, whose name is Jaap Buth, was elected Honorary Secretary.

In order to make progress, there was clearly a need to muster support for the Board from as many countries of the European Union as possible including those with established vascular specialities that had previously been reluctant to get involved. So I spent a good deal of time flying around speaking at national society annual congresses and various ad hoc meetings. France and Spain, in particular were reluctant to engage. I had excellent personal relationships with many vascular surgeons in France, where the speciality had been established for years but they had their own international French language society to which they gave priority. At least, they were polite whereas in Spain the attitude was, at times, frankly hostile. On one occasion, I addressed a large meeting in Barcelona. Margaret Thatcher had just been bashing European Union Commissioners with her metaphorical handbag and had come away with a substantial rebate. When I finished speaking, a man at the back of the auditorium, clearly irate, stood up and shouted, "How dare Mr Harris come here to lecture us about vascular surgery after Mrs Thatcher?" I am still not sure exactly what he meant, but I got the impression that he considered us Brits to be disgraceful Europeans; and, in any case, as someone from a Country in which vascular surgery was an under-developed non-speciality, what did I know about anything?

The Aosta Group was not the only organisation pressing for recognition of vascular surgery as a speciality in Europe. In 1987, at a meeting at Charing Cross Hospital in London, a new European Society of Vascular Surgery (ESVS) had been inaugurated. Roger Greenhalgh had successfully garnered support from the national representative bodies of vascular surgery of most parts of Europe, including countries that were not members of the European Union. France was again, a notable exception. The principal aim of The ESVS was to act as a forum for debate of the clinical, academic and scientific aspects of vascular surgery.

But, the membership, especially those at the top, had vested interests also in the politics of promoting vascular surgery as a speciality. Following in the wake of the Aosta initiative, the leaders of the ESVS made a decision to add their weight to the cause in the personage of Professor Roger Greenhalgh himself.

Roger was destined for greatness. There could never have been any doubt about it in his own mind. With this certain knowledge came not only the obligation to put in the hours of hard work necessary to achieve greatness but also a license to do whatever it takes. In these respects, he was much like many other 'great' men whose less attractive qualities are widely recognised, but tend to be overlooked in favour of the benefits conferred upon society at large by their obsessional drive to achieve greatness. To add to his self-inflicted trials, Roger has had to overcome serious health issues including kidney failure for which he eventually had a successful transplant. Over the years, inflammation in his spine has caused his back to become rounded and his neck stiff with a forward inclination obliging him to turn his whole body to look around. These features together, with a certain corpulence have given him a distinctly Churchillian bearing. Unfortunately, any pretension he may have in this regard is undermined by a high-pitched, squeaky voice which contrasts unfavourably with Winston Churchill's famously characteristic growl.

Roger was in rude physical health in 1977, when he and I first met, as shortlisted candidates for the Chair of Surgery at Charing Cross Hospital Medical School. At the time, I was stumbling along from one day to the next, hoping to land a job as a consultant vascular surgeon somewhere, sometime without any serious pretensions about being a professor. But, as the incumbent senior registrar on the professorial unit, I was encouraged to apply. Roger, on the other hand, knew exactly what he wanted and he knew how to get it.

Naturally he got the job.

The quest for speciality recognition of vascular surgery was just one arena that brought me back into contact with him. Typically, having determined that the Section of General Surgery was where the power lay regarding the fate of the vascular surgery in the EU, he exercised his considerable political skills to get himself appointed as the UK representative. The Subsection and Board of Vascular Surgery were already established by this time and, as President of these bodies, I was an ex-officio member of the Section of General Surgery also. Predictably, following in the wake of the success of vascular surgery in achieving Board status, the Section was inundated with demands from its other subspecialties, such as breast and bowel surgery, to be afforded the same privileges. In response Roger came up with the idea of a federation of surgical specialities sharing a 'common trunk' of basic surgical training all under the continued governance of the Section of General Surgery. He christened his concept, the 'surgical envelope'. Although, he pushed the envelope very hard, things did not work out quite as he envisaged because, within a relatively short time, all the important subdivisions of general surgery were awarded Speciality Section status and were no longer governed by the Section of General Surgery. This included vascular surgery. Roger was not deterred. In 1998, he was elected President of the Section of General Surgery and, in 2002, President of the Board of General Surgery. Finally, he was made 'Honorary Life President of the European Board of Vascular Surgery'.

Immediately after the Board of Vascular Surgery had been launched in 1994, we began work to organise Board examinations. Under European Union law, professional certification required for statutory licensing of doctors is devolved to national examination authorities and cannot be usurped by any European-wide initiative. In the UK, the Royal Colleges are the responsible bodies for setting specialist examinations and the General Medical Council is the licensing authority. The problem, from a European harmonisation point of view, is that all national institutions have histories and traditions stretching back hundreds of years with established idiosyncrasies that they are unwilling to compromise. For this reason, any attempt to standardise examinations across Europe was a non-starter. The aim of the European Board Assessments was to appeal directly to trainees to conform to agreed standards over the heads of the national institutions. Board certification would be offered as a voluntary addition to the national qualification which would retain statutory priority.

Rather than seeking academic excellence, our aim was to identify candidates with the requisite diagnostic skills and decision-making abilities for safe specialist practice. Accordingly, we developed a competency-based form of assessment. This is an approach which has since been adopted almost universally by national examination boards but, at that time, was a relatively novel concept. Aspiring candidates, first had to pass an eligibility test (Part 1), which was a paper exercise, based upon accredited logbook records. These records, immediately exposed grossly uneven standards within the EU. In Italy, for example, you could become a specialist vascular surgeon without having done a single operation. In the UK, despite the fact that vascular surgery was not a recognised speciality, candidates with speciality qualifications in general surgery had performed large numbers of vascular operations, including major ones under the supervision of their consultant. The criterion we set for progression to Part 2 was that the candidate had to have undertaken a minimum of 400 operative procedures accumulated over a minimum period of five years with a substantial number as the lead surgeon under supervision. Those who met this minimum standard were then invited to attend for individual assessment by members of an international examination board under the chairmanship of Professor Bernard Nachbur from Bern in Switzerland. The format of Part 2 was a series of viva voce examinations based upon actual clinical case records and diagnostic images. Later, we introduced tasks performed on operating simulators to test manual dexterity and technical skills.

The first European Board of Vascular Surgery Assessments took place in Venice in 1996 alongside the annual congress of the ESVS. Of 103 applicants, only 15 satisfied the Part 1 eligibility criteria and, of these, 13 succeeded in passing the Part 2 assessments. From this very modest beginning, the number of candidates increased year on year with a rising pass rate. Although the examinations were set and the candidates were assessed entirely, independently by the Board of Vascular Surgery, we had not escaped completely from the shadow of the Section and Board of General Surgery. For the first ten years, successful candidates were awarded European Board of Surgery Qualification in Vascular Surgery (EBSQvasc) certificates. In 2005, vascular surgery finally satisfied all requirements for recognition as an independent surgical speciality and the qualification became Fellowship of the European Board of Vascular Surgery (FEBVS). It has remained faithful to the principle of competency assessment and as it has grown progressively in importance, it has been adopted and accepted by some European Union Countries as the statutory qualification for speciality licensing in vascular surgery.

By 1996, the groundwork for formal recognition of vascular surgery as an independent speciality was laid. European-wide registries of vascular procedures and dissemination of 'best-practice' would follow with immense benefits for patients and the ability of vascular surgeons to work anywhere in the EU irrespective of their member state of origin was significantly enhanced. Domenico Palombo's vision was well on the way to being realised and our Aosta Group jaunts to the tiny village of Saint Vincent, with its dubious night time diversions high in the Italian Alps, came to an end.

Chapter 7
Julian Brookes

Before disaster struck, things had been going well for Julian Brookes. At the age of 34, he was already a partner in a firm of Liverpool solicitors.

Specialising in commercial law, his professional abilities were beginning to be acknowledged well beyond the confines of the city. He thrived on the pressure of work and was happy to put in the long hours required to sustain his growing reputation. Tall and fit, he favoured classical dark suits for the office but defied the usual conservative dress code of his genre with an eclectic collection of colourful ties and rebellious longish dark brown hair which despite constantly being raked back with his fingers, flopped down over his eyes. He took care to look after himself; did not smoke, rarely drank during the week and, work permitting, played squash at The Racquet Club close by his office in the lunch breaks or at the end of the day. He also liked to run, which he did mainly at weekends. He discovered, early in his adult life, that exercise-induced endorphins were an effective means of relieving stress, when the going got tough. Running had become an important part of his coping strategy. Although personable, and often engaging on subjects that interested him, frivolous small talk did not come easily to Julian. He seemed to lack social confidence at times but in reality, it was obsession with his work that made him seem withdrawn. He was overly ambitious. Self-induced pressure combined with high intelligence was a source of strength and his professional success, but it was also his weakness. Over-committed and tired, he frequently came across as self-absorbed and detached and those who did not know him well often thought him arrogant. Not that such perceptions troubled Julian too much.

His beautiful wife, two years his junior, was slim and vivacious with blue eyes and the most gorgeous thick red hair, which she usually kept tied back with a clip or a bow. Originally from London, she had a French mother who gave her the name Janine. She was also a lawyer. Her expertise was intellectual property. She worked in the Liverpool office of a well-known UK firm of patent attorneys. She met Julian at a Liverpool Law Society dinner and within weeks, she had moved in with him at his bachelor flat in a converted warehouse at the Albert Dock. After nearly two years of living together there, in relatively cramped conditions, they bought a sizeable detached house, with a small garden, at Heswall on the Wirral and got married. But, with both of them preoccupied, with their careers on upward trajectories, neither was ready to stop working, so they put off having children for a couple of years at least. That was two years before 'the turning point'.

Julian's domain was the legal conference room where he was in his element and totally in control. Confident, well-prepared and engaging, he was an articulate and persuasive negotiator; invariably polite and patient. However, on that fateful day in February 1996, his patience and control deserted him in a big way. He was in the midst of one of those recurring phases in which he had simply taken on too much work. Janine was away in London, on business, and in her absence, he had worked at home late into the previous night on a report that was already several weeks overdue. There was an enormous pile of documents to wade through and when he finally packed up, at 3 am, he had not even begun to put together a first draft from his copious notes. His head ached and his brain would no longer function properly. On previous occasions, when he had worked late into the night under similar circumstances, he had not felt quite so completely exhausted, and he wondered if he had picked up a flu bug. Whatever, he was desperate for sleep. As he crawled into bed he resolved to go for a run soon. Sleep did not come quickly and he passed another fitful hour tossing and turning before finally drifting into oblivion.

At 8.30 am, he jolted wide-awake in a state of panic. Daylight was flooding into the room. His eyes hurt and his head was throbbing. He was late! Very late! Having dressed hurriedly without shaving or showering, he hit the road at peak rush hour. A queue of exasperatingly slow-moving traffic was heading towards the Mersey tunnel. There was no other way for him to get to the city centre and to his office. He slotted into a gap in the queue of vehicles and sat there tapping impatiently at the steering wheel with his wedding ring as he crawled towards the pay barriers at the entrance to the tunnel. As usual, when time was short, he managed, perversely, to select the slowest moving queue. Infuriated, he thought about changing lanes and then didn't. His mouth was dry. He had had nothing to eat or drink and there was no let-up in the persistent throbbing in his head. He decided, he just had to go with the flow. He was going to be horribly late, in any case.

Already waiting in his office was an eminent lawyer who had travelled up from London that morning accompanied by his junior. They were there, representing a construction company. His own client, a wealthy businessman, was investing in a building development to be undertaken in Liverpool by this company and Julian's job was to negotiate the contract. If he got it right, it could be worth a lot of money to his client but it was a standard matter and Julian had not anticipated serious problems. A few sticking points remained to be settled and this was the purpose of the meeting but the principles of the agreement were in place. With just a few minor amendments to propose on his client's behalf, he had considered the two hours that had been scheduled first thing in the morning would be more than sufficient time. But, one hour had already passed from the appointed start time and he was not feeling good.

As he hurried into the conference room, followed by his articled clerk who carried the bundle of documents, the visitors were sat at one end of the table. The atmosphere was not welcoming. Julian's proffered handshakes and profuse apologies were met by the senior of the two lawyers with a perfunctory "OK. These things happen. Let's just get on with it, shall we?" They rearranged themselves facing each other at opposite sides in the middle of the long conference table. Julian poured himself a cup of coffee from a thermos jug on a tray that had been placed between them and added two heaped teaspoons of sugar. Mindful of the risk of aggravating an already rancorous situation, he determined not to be affronted by the lack of civility. After all, it was he, not them, who was at fault. They had managed to arrive from London in time on the early train. Confident that, once into his flow, everything would settle down and agreement would soon follow, he began to lay out his case as politely and as respectfully as he could manage under the circumstances. However, it soon became clear that the other side was in no mood to compromise. Whether, they were just irritated by the delay or executing a planned strategy with some other purpose in mind, was not clear but Julian found himself unable to make any headway. No reasoned arguments for debate or rebuttal were offered by the other side, rather just an unequivocal "no." The attitude of the elder man conveyed, to Julian, the impression that he considered him too inexperienced and lightweight to waste time with explanations of points of law or self-evident truths. After an hour of futile exchanges had passed without appreciable progress, Julian was struggling increasingly to maintain a calm demeanour. His patience was running out and as his frustration intensified into anger, he first developed a horrible sensation that something was not right. Then the pain came. Suddenly and violently, deep in his chest and through to the centre of back, as though a knife had been plunged into his body and twisted. A sick feeling rose in his stomach and his heart was thumping in his chest in time with the thumping in his head. He was entering totally uncharted territory as rising panic replaced his normal rational thought processes. He had to escape. The senior lawyer, looking at him over the top of half-moon glasses, was repeating once again that Julian's proposal was unacceptable to their client and that was all he needed to know. Interrupting him abruptly, Julian lifted his hand in a 'stop' gesture and in a low, almost whispered voice said, "Sorry. I need some air." He stood up and almost overbalanced as he knocked over his chair. Then he headed quickly for the door. Nobody protested. A glance at Julian's face, which was deathly white, said it all. Once outside, he made for the toilet but halfway across the outer office he stumbled and fell to the floor. Secretaries sat at their desks heard a groan and saw him crumple to the ground. The nightmare had begun!

At the Royal, Julian was conscious but in agony as paramedics rushed him into A&E Majors on a trolley. He could barely speak due to the pain. His breathing was constricted. His blood pressure was high, very high in fact, at 230/120. The first thought of the junior doctor who examined him on arrival was 'heart attack' but, other than confirming a very rapid heart rate, the electrocardiogram (ECG) was normal. A chest X-ray also failed to show anything very obvious, at least to the junior doctor. However, a radiologist seeing the films straight away organised an emergency CT scan of the heart and blood vessels. And, the diagnosis was clear. Julian's life was in grave danger and he was in urgent need of surgery.

The seeds of Julian's dire state were sown at his conception. A genetic aberration, the result of a random quirk of fate, had given him a fatally weakened aorta. Silently, it had been yielding step by step to the pressure of the blood inside it, progressively dilating it until, on that stressful day in his thirty-fifth year, it had given way. Had it burst completely; he would have died instantly. As it was, he was hanging on to life by a thread. What had happened was that the inner lining of the aorta had torn, close to the point, where it emerged from the heart and through this tear a jet of blood had stripped a completely new channel within the wall along the whole length of the aorta, in his chest and down into his abdomen. At this stage the blood was still contained, just! Without surgery, rupture was inevitable at the weakest point close to the heart with rapid death, the only possible outcome. This might occur within days, hours, minutes or even seconds. The timing was impossible to predict. Following a number of frantic 'phone calls, an intravenous infusion was administered through a drip to lower the pressure of the blood in the aorta and he was transferred, at speed, by ambulance with blue lights flashing and sirens blaring to the cardiothoracic centre (CTC) at Broadgreen Hospital.

Julian had his first bit of luck that day because standing by at the CTC was someone who knew as much as anyone, anywhere, about aortic dissections. His name was Abbas Rashid. Abbas was the senior cardiothoracic surgeon at the CTC and an aortic expert. A thoroughly delightful man of Iraqi origin, he had been first assistant to the irascible Ben Meade when I arrived in Liverpool in 1979 and upon the retirement of his boss, he had taken over as chief. He had, what I would describe as a southern-European personality although, coming as he did from the Middle East, I suspect his character was typical of most well-disposed people from that part of the world. He either loved you or he didn't. It was black or white. Those he loved, he would greet with a generous bear hug and kisses. If he disliked you, it was equally obvious. He liked me. And I liked him back, in my reserved English manner. Consequently, we got on well and we carried out operations together on many aortas. He looked after the heart and the top end, while I took care of the abdominal part below.

For Abbas, emergency operations on patients with acute dissection of the aorta were commonplace. I was not involved with Julian's first operation that day, and the first to save his life, but others would follow. The breast-bone was split down the middle with a saw to expose the root of the aorta as it emerged from the heart and the torn section was cut away to be replaced with a tube of matching size made from Dacron material. While the stitching was being done, a mechanical pump kept the blood circulating to the brain and other vital organs. It was a big operation but one that Abbas had well worked out and one that, barring technical mishaps, was predicted to succeed in a fit young man like Julian. He did, indeed, make a good recovery and was well enough to get back to work six weeks later. Unfortunately, that was not to be the end of the matter.

The problem for Julian, and for many like him, was that this first operation, though life-saving, could not address the damage caused to the rest of the aorta by the dissection. The whole structure, already weak from birth, was now even weaker. Blood continued to flow through it to the rest of the body but where, originally, there had been just one channel, there were now two. It was double-barrelled with the original and the new 'false' channel side by side, spiralling around each other. Some parts of the body and the internal organs were fed by one of the channels and some by the other. Medication was prescribed to keep his blood pressure low in order to minimise the strain on the weakened vessel but, despite this, the wall of new 'false' channel continued to stretch progressively. As it did so, it compressed the original, 'true' channel narrowing it and threatening to cut off the blood supply to some of his organs. And as the wall of the 'false' channel stretched, it became thinner like an inflating balloon with a renewed threat that it would burst with massive, most probably fatal, internal bleeding.

So, two years after the first operation, I got a call from Abbas. The whole of the remaining aorta would have to be replaced. By any standards, this was going to be a massive undertaking and the stakes could not have been higher. At the age of just 36 years, Julian faced certain death within the next couple of years without surgery. Yet, there was a one in ten chance, that he would not survive the surgery and a similar risk that, if he did survive, he would be left with life-changing complications. The most devastating complication of massive aortic surgery is paraplegia; paralysis of both legs usually accompanied by bowel and urinary incontinence. The severe disability that results is life-long and, for many, a fate worse than death itself. Julian and Janine fully understood these risks and, like most others in their situation concluded that surgery with an 80 percent chance of survival without serious complications was preferable to certain death.

So, at 8 o'clock on a February morning in 1998, Abbas and I sat in the theatre rest room at the cardiothoracic centre drinking coffee and watching early morning TV on the BBC while keeping an eye on a wall-mounted screen displaying Julian's vital functions that were being transmitted from the operating theatre where the anaesthetic team were working to get him ready for surgery. This was a complicated process that took the best part of two hours. Tubes of various sorts were inserted into every orifice, multiple drips were set up and pressure monitors were manipulated into his heart, his arteries, his veins and into the spinal canal. There was an electrocardiograph to monitor his heart rhythm an electroencephalograph to monitor his brain waves and a double-barrelled tube in his windpipe to enable one lung to be collapsed while the other remained ventilated. While the anaesthetic team worked on Julian's body, the pump technician, John, set up the heart-lung machine. The nurses sorted and counted a large array of surgical instruments and laid them out on two trolleys covered with sterile green towels. Altogether, ten people were involved in these preparations, eleven including Julian who, asleep at the centre of the activity, was completely oblivious to it all. Sometime before 10 o'clock, Abbas and I got the message they were ready for us. The ambiance seemed calm and relaxed as we entered the theatre, one of the anaesthetists was recounting a story about losing his keys and being locked out of his house but, beneath the apparent levity, there was tension in the air, unspoken anxiety about what the next few hours might have in store. The heart monitor beeped rhythmically and the suckers hissed softly in readiness.

The aorta arises from the heart immediately behind the breastbone. It then, loops over to the left and backwards, before passing vertically down the back of the chest on the left side of the spine and entering the abdomen through an opening in the diaphragm. Roughly, at the level of the belly button, it splits into two with a branch for each leg. It is the sole channel supplying blood to the entire body and all its organs save for the lungs. The first challenge to be overcome in replacing it, is how to reach it. Most surgery on the torso is confined, either to the chest or the abdomen. Exposure of the entire length of the aorta requires the longest of surgical incisions starting from the back of the upper left chest, running around and across the lower edge of the rib cage and then, onto the front of the abdomen and all the way down to the pubis. Julian's body was twisted on the operating table in order to open up this long spiral wound as you might open up a tube of cardboard from a toilet roll or a Pringles container. Making this incision and laying open the chest and abdominal cavities while sealing or tying the bleeding points took the best part of an hour.

In theory, the chest was Abbas' territory and the abdomen, mine; but we worked together assisting each other in both areas. Once inside, blood was drawn from the heart via plastic tubing into the heart-lung machine and pumped back through two other tubes, one entering the groin to supply the lower part of the body and the other the neck to supply only the brain. In this way, circulation to the vital organs was maintained while there was no blood flowing through the aorta. As it passed through the pumps, it was cooled in a carefully controlled way to give added protection to vital organs.

All of that done, we were ready to start work on the aorta itself in order to replace it with a Dacron fabric tube. Along its length, the aorta gives rise to branches carrying blood to all parts of the body. These must be connected into the new fabric aorta. Some are more important than others, and it is not just a matter of size. In the lower chest, a very small branch, called the artery of Adamkiewicz, supplies the spinal cord. Permanent exclusion of this vessel is likely to result in paraplegia and it is of the utmost importance to connect it into the graft. Actually the artery of Adamkiewicz cannot be seen at operation. It does not arise directly from the aorta itself but from one of the intercostal arteries in the lower chest. The problem is that it is not always the same intercostal artery. Therefore a patch of the aorta bearing the openings into all the intercostal arteries in the lower part of the chest has to be connected to the graft. While the patch is being stitched in place blood flow into the intercostal arteries, and therefore the artery of Adamkiewicz, has to be temporarily arrested so the job has to be completed quickly and it is not an easy task.

Just below the diaphragm, a number of big branches arise close together to supply the abdominal organs; the liver, the spleen, the kidneys and the intestines. Two patches of the wall of the aorta bearing the openings into these branches also needed to be stitched into matching holes cut in the Dacron graft to accommodate them. One of the patches bore branches to the liver, the spleen and the right kidney, and the other, the branch to the left kidney alone. Julian's anatomy was unusual in that there were two arteries supplying the liver instead of just one. This was not a problem at this point, both being included in the first patch. However, it would prove to be a source of significant technical problems later in his story.

All proceeded according to plan without any untoward events. Just after 2 o'clock, we took it in turns to each have a five-minute break with a visit to the loo followed by a quick snack and a drink. By 6 o'clock the job was done and we were almost ready to close up. Before we did so we had to be sure that all internal bleeding had stopped and we spent a good 30 minutes checking and rechecking for bleeding points before pulling together the gaping hole in Julian's torso. Sometime after 7 o'clock, we were back in the theatre rest room watching the television as the anaesthetic team prepared him for transfer to the intensive care unit. He would remain asleep and on a ventilator until tomorrow morning, at least. We settled into comfortable chairs with cups of coffee and put our feet up thinking we had done a good days work.

I had been asleep for about half an hour when the telephone rang shortly after midnight. It was the anaesthetic senior registrar from the intensive care unit.

"About your patient, Julian Seabrook. Just thought you should know, he is losing blood from his abdominal drain at a steady rate of about 120 mils an hour. We are replacing it and giving him clotting factors but he is now on his eighth pint of blood since theatre."

"OK," I say. "Thanks for letting me know. Let's see if the rate reduces with the clotting factors. Call me back in a couple of hours, if not." Three hours later, the telephone rang again.

"Sorry. The rate of blood loss reduced slightly for a time but we think this may have related to a fall in his blood pressure. The pressure has come up again with fluid replacement and now he is losing at more than 100 mils an hour again. It's coming from the abdominal drain. The chest drains are dry."

"OK," I say. "I'm coming in. Make preparations to take him back to the operating room."

Julian was already on the operating table when I walked into the theatre, 30 minutes later. The cardiac monitor was beeping at a rate that was far too fast and there were frequent bursts of erratic rhythm. Sharp, no-nonsense, communications between the staff betrayed a high level of anxiety. Nurses were running around collecting together and counting instruments and getting the suckers and other paraphernalia together. Julian's exposed belly was grossly swollen and, when I put my hand upon it, it was tight as a drum. In addition to the 120 mils of blood an hour, that had come out of the plastic tube draining his abdomen, there were many litres more trapped inside. His blood pressure had crashed. His skin was very white. The anaesthetists were squeezing bags of blood into drips in his arm and neck. There was no urine in the bag connected to his bladder and it looked as if the kidneys had shut down. Julian was in big trouble, but he was young and fit and there was every chance that, when we had found and arrested the source of the bleeding, he would bounce back quickly.

Manoj, the Indian senior registrar, prepped Julian's abdomen while I donned a plastic apron and scrubbed up. The stitches holding the abdomen together were under great tension due to the pressure of the blood inside and as we cut them, the wound gave way, releasing a flood of watery blood, which poured onto the floor followed by huge globules of soft, black jelly clots. Two litres of fluid collected into the sucker bottles in no time at all, and there was considerably more than this in the expanding, slippery puddle around our feet. When we managed to get a view inside, we could see a pool of blood in the depths, which filled back up again quickly, each time we sucked it away. There was no single bleeding point to be seen. Blood just seemed to be oozing from all the dissected surfaces. We packed the area with surgical swabs to soak up the ooze and waited for five minutes or so while the anaesthetists worked to regain control of Julian's blood pressure. They were more successful than before because the pressure of blood in the abdomen had been pushing up the diaphragm to compress the heart and lungs and this had now been released. The 15th and 16th pints of blood, since completion of the earlier surgery, were being transfused together with more clotting factors. One of the problems associated with massive haemorrhage is that the constituents from which blood clots are formed and which are essential to nature's own mechanism for arresting bleeding, get used up and, unless replaced, the bleeding will never stop. When we removed the packs to take another look, we could see more clearly the Dacron aorta with the two patches of original aortic wall bearing branches to the abdominal organs. There were numerous small bleeding points which we stitched or sealed with diathermy and after an hour or so the bleeding was reduced. Not totally dry, but better. The anaesthetists were also happier. So, we decided to close up again and return Julian to the intensive care unit. I went home for a quick shower and breakfast before returning to start the routine work of the day in the outpatient clinic.

Just after 11 o'clock that same morning, the clinic nurse interrupted me while examining a patient to say that someone from the cardiac surgery intensive care unit was on the 'phone and wanted to speak to me urgently. It was Glen, the senior anaesthetist. He said, "You need to take another look at Julian. The bleeding slowed for a time after last night's op but there's a hundred mils of blood or more an hour coming from the abdominal drain again and he's needing a lot of fluid to keep his pressure up. He's had 22 litres of blood altogether now. He's OK at the moment but we're not going to able to keep him going at this rate."

"OK Glen," I say. "Thanks for letting me know. I'll come over as soon as I've finished here."

Glen was right, pouring blood in at one end while it poured out the other, was not going to end well. Janine was sitting by Julian's bed, holding his hand, when I arrived. Julian was oblivious, still unconscious on a ventilator surrounded by bloody drips, bloody drains, catheters and erratically beeping and flashing alarms and monitors. His swollen tongue partly protruded from his mouth alongside a large plastic tube connecting him to the rhythmically hissing ventilator and held in place with a bandage around his neck. His unblinking eyes were covered with pads of paraffin gauze to protect against drying and ulceration of the cornea. He did not look pretty and there was no disguising that his condition was critical. Janine was both horrified and distraught. I did my best to be reassuring as I explained that we just needed to find and stop the source of bleeding and he would be fine. This meant another operation but he still had an excellent chance of complete recovery. She was not convinced. With barely suppressed hostility, she said, "If it is that simple, why have you not done it so far and what are you going to do differently this time?" In truth, I did not know. There was no blood at all in the chest drains. All the bleeding was from the abdomen. Therefore, I deduced that the source had to be below the diaphragm. There had to be a breach in the stitching in the aorta or a torn blood vessel hidden in there, somewhere. But where? And why hadn't we found it? We could not stop now. To do nothing was not an option. We had to get him back to theatre quickly once more and take another look.

At 4 o'clock, Julian was on the operating table for the third time in two days and we began again to search for the source of the blood which was still welling up from the depths. After another two hours of repeatedly looking, stitching and cauterising and then packing and waiting, there was nothing more that I could think of to do. And then, we noticed a small tear on the surface of the spleen. It was not a big tear and, as we watched, the bleeding from it was not great. It was not certain, either, whether the tear had just happened or been there all along since the first operation. Lying under the ribs and the diaphragm on the left side of the abdominal cavity, it had to be moved to gain access to the aorta. It is a soft, fragile organ full of blood and very vulnerable to injury by metal retractors. We had previously checked it multiple times without finding anything, but maybe we just missed seeing this small tear. The spleen is not essential for survival and the safest thing under the circumstances was to remove it. This definitely eliminated any possibility of further bleeding from this source. But as I struggled again to close the gaping hole in Julian's abdomen, I could not shake off a strong underlying sense of anxiety that it was not yet the end of his problems. The 33rd pint of blood transfusion dripped steadily into his veins.

Back home, I had some supper and went to bed expecting the phone to ring any minute. But it didn't ring. So, I did not wake until the radio alarm went off at 6.30 am as normal. I called the intensive care unit for an update hoping for the best but fearing the worst. He was alive but still bleeding. My heart sank. They were keeping pace with blood transfusions and additional fluid replacement and it had been decided, there was no point calling me as there was nothing more that could conceivably be done at that time. However, he had now had 40 units of blood plus enormous quantities of other blood products. The blood bank was running out of supplies and struggling to find more. It was clear, a decision would have to be made whether to continue or to withdraw active treatment. Very few people survive a transfusion of this magnitude and there were signs that Julian's internal organs were starting to fail. It was looking very unlikely that he could recover, even if, by some miracle, the bleeding did stop. I called Abbas and we agreed to meet with the anaesthetists at 10 o'clock in the intensive care unit to make a decision.

Nobody was in favour of another 'blind' operation, that is to say, opening up Julian's abdomen again without any clear objective indication as to where the bleeding was coming from. An X-ray could possibly provide this information. I felt the unspoken criticism for not having requested this the day before, and now it may be too late, but this is what we decided to do. The anaesthetists were fairly certain that Julian would not come through a fourth major surgical intervention but everyone agreed that he should be given this one last chance. It was also agreed that, in the absence of information to guide further intervention, active therapy would be withdrawn. Janine having lost all confidence in us and no longer able to watch her husband's apparently unstoppable demise, was nowhere to be seen.

The X-rays explained everything. The source of the bleeding was not in the abdomen but in the chest!

Julian's surgery did not entail removal of the aorta. It had been opened up along its length and left in place with the new replacement Dacron tube laid inside it. Up in the chest, pairs of branches, the intercostal arteries, arise from the aorta and run between the ribs on each side of the body to supply the muscles, skin and bones. The intercostal arteries in the lower part of the chest, one of which gives rise to the artery of Adamkiewicz to the spinal cord, had been joined into the graft at the first operation. But, those higher up in the chest are dispensable and they had been simply closed off individually with stitches. One of these stitches was defective and blood was spurting back into the space between the residual native aorta and the graft, then tracking down alongside the graft through the diaphragm to emerge into the abdominal cavity. None of this could be seen from within the abdomen itself, just blood welling up from nowhere in particular at the bottom end.

The X-ray images showed all of this clearly. They also showed a possible route to achieve what I had singularly failed to achieve without need for another major operation. It would not be easy, far from it, but if a catheter could be introduced into the bleeding vessel, it might be possible to block it with a plug. The interventional radiologist on duty for emergencies that day was Derek Gould. He did a brilliant job. Through a needle inserted through Julian's back, under X-ray guidance, he manipulated a fine catheter into the space between the new and the old aorta and into the mouth of the bleeding artery. Through this catheter, he injected coils of fine wire. Specifically designed to plug small arteries the wires are coated with a fluffy fabric that quickly causes the blood to clot around them. The bleeding was immediately arrested by this procedure and Julian bounced back remarkably as a result. A corner had been turned. But that was still not the end of the saga of Julian Brookes! Not by a long way!

For the time being things settled down. He left hospital three weeks later, and three months after that returned to work, on a part-time basis. Having been made acutely aware of his tenuous hold on life, his priorities changed. Career progression was no longer top of the list. He and Janine consulted a geneticist and received the welcome news that his condition was not inherited and would not be passed onto their off-spring.

He attended a follow-up clinic at the cardio-thoracic centre at regular intervals for scans to monitor his graft and, for a time, all was well. Then, after 18 months or so, there were clear signs that the patches of natural aorta connected into the graft were themselves starting to stretch. Within another six months, the one with branches to the liver and right kidney was the size of a golf ball and there was a substantial and growing risk that it would burst. Janine had given birth to a son, six months previously and the stakes for Julian were now higher than ever. The surgical challenges involved in dealing with this situation were greater, even than those of the first operation. The patch would have to be exposed once more in the depths of the abdomen in order to remove it and each individual branch would then need to be reconnected into the circulation somehow. This was uncharted territory and dense scar tissue from his previous operations would increase the hazards considerably. The chances of something going wrong were exceptionally high.

The dread on the faces of Julian and Janine at the prospect of another operation said it all. The nightmare, they had thought was behind them, had returned. Understandably, fear of surgery had been indelibly implanted in their shared psyche and it was clear, they would need time to come to terms with this new situation. So, we boosted Julian's medication to reduce his blood pressure further and awaited their decision.

It was about 1 o'clock in the morning, approximately three weeks after that consultation, when the telephone rang. The voice on the other end of the line said, "Julian Brookes has just been admitted to A & E. He's in a bad state. Sudden onset of severe abdominal and back pain. He's conscious but his blood pressure's only 60 systolic. He's getting lots of fluid and we're waiting for cross-matched blood." The patch had burst!

An hour later, he was anaesthetised and on an operating table, once more, with blood being pumped into his neck and arms and surrounded by beeping machines. The sense of deja-vu was very real. I did not know what I was going to do, what it would take to stop the bleeding or if I would get him off the table alive. One thing that was certain was that he would certainly die very soon if we did nothing. There was nothing to lose.

On opening his belly, we were met, as expected, by dense scar tissue binding his intestines together and forming a mass obstructing access to the aorta that, at first, seemed impenetrable. Eventually, a small channel did open up through which I could see blood spurting rhythmically through a tear of about two centimetres in the side of the bigger patch that included branches to the liver and right kidney but no longer the spleen, which had been removed. Comprehensive reconstruction with implantation of the individual branches into the aorta was going to be technically impossible under the circumstances in which we found ourselves. The best we could hope for, was to stop the bleeding by any means, and get him off the operating table alive. Through the narrow channel and down a deep hole, access was extremely difficult and a clear view unattainable but eventually we managed to get a clamp across the tear and stitch it. When the clamp came off, there was no longer a jet of blood and the branches arising from the patch seemed to be intact and filling nicely with blood. We all heaved a collective sigh of relief and I closed him up, grateful to get him off the operating table alive.

Julian bounced back quickly once more from this latest tussle with death. However, we had done no more than cobble together the tear in the patch. The patch was still there becoming increasingly attenuated as it continued stretch inexorably in response the pressure of blood within it. It was like a time-bomb ticking away towards a final terminal explosion.

But Julian did not die. In fact he lived to see his little boy grow up and to pursue a happy family life. What it was that denied the grim reaper and changed Julian's destiny, we shall see in the next chapter.

Chapter 8
Epiphany

Sometime in 1990 Carlos Menem, the President of Argentina, contacted Juan Parodi, a vascular surgeon working in Buenos Aires, with a special request. The President had heard that Parodi was researching an idea for treating abdominal aortic aneurysms by means of a minimally invasive procedure designed to avoid the risks of major surgery. The idea was to take a fabric graft, much like those that were stitched in place in conventional open operations, and compress it inside a long tube of small enough diameter, to be entered into the femoral artery in the groin. Guided by X-ray images on a screen, the tube containing the graft would be threaded through the arterial system into the aorta and, once in place, the graft would be extruded to open up as an inner tube to line the inside of the aorta. In this way, the aneurysm would be isolated and protected from the internal pressure that threatened to cause it to burst. Making this idea workable, necessitated the addition of something to ensure that the fabric tube would open up fully and also to hold it in place. In 1985, a Texan radiologist by the name of Julio Palmaz had invented a metal stent for treatment of blocked or narrowed arteries. It was essentially, a wire cage that was compressed tightly over an uninflated balloon on the end of a long catheter. Introduced through a needle into the arterial tree, it was guided by X-ray imaging into the blockage and expanded by inflating the balloon, which was then, withdrawn. After expansion, the stent formed a rigid structure that was left in place to hold the artery open. The Palmaz stent had been designed for treatment of diseased small arteries. Parodi approached the inventor with the idea of scaling it up in size, in order to adapt it for the purpose, he had in mind. Palmaz agreed to work with him and they collaborated together to make a prototype device. It had an extra-large stent attached to one end of a large diameter fabric graft. By 1990, they had deployed these prototypes successfully in animal models but never in humans.

A close friend of the President had a large abdominal aortic aneurysm and had been told, it would soon kill him. He also had a bad heart and severe breathing problems which prohibited conventional surgical treatment. So, the President, on hearing about Parodi's work, contacted him to request that he treat the friend with this new invention. I have no idea, how the conversation went and whether, or how much, pressure was applied to Parodi but he agreed to perform the operation. The patient survived and history was made with repercussions for vascular surgery around the world.

Endovascular aneurysm repair (EVAR), as the procedure later became known, was an idea whose time had come. In 1987, totally unknown to Parodi, who was still experimenting on animals in Buenos Aires, a Ukrainian surgeon called Nicolas Volodos had treated a patient with an aneurysm of the thoracic aorta using a very similar endovascular device. Few people knew about it, and certainly nobody in the English-speaking western world, because although Volodos described his operation in a scientific paper, it was published in an obscure, Russian language journal. Also, in the late 1980s, a young British born vascular research fellow, called Tim Chuter, was developing prototypes at Columbia University Hospital in New York. These luminaries, each working entirely independently of each other, had come up with very similar solutions to the same problem. Their collective idea was a logical iteration of developments in minimally invasive endovascular technologies that had been evolving over the previous decade. Parodi, who published a report of his first operation in an English language journal in 1991, got most of the credit, but as so often in these situations, he was not the first.

I had no inkling about any of these developments until, in 1990, sitting in the sumptuous ballroom of the splendid Art-Deco Waldorf Astoria Hotel in New York, along with two or three thousand other attendees at the Annual Veith Vascular Symposium, I had an epiphany moment. Moving X-ray images were being projected onto a giant screen. They showed a prototype aortic endograft being deployed into the aorta of a dog. The video was presented by Professor Richard Green who was Tim Chuter's boss at Columbia. Juan Parodi's report had not yet been published. It was a revelation! One that would have a major impact on my future surgical practice; and one, that ten years later, would give Julian Brookes the chance of living long enough to see his little boy grow up.

For years, I had been painfully mindful of the need for a better alternative to brutal, dangerous conventional surgery for treatment of aortic aneurysms. There was no certainty that this was it, but it seemed to me, there was a good chance it could be; and, on the night flight back across the Atlantic, I determined to get involved with this new technology. The question was how to go about it? If an aortic endograft can be introduced into the aorta of a dog, as the video had demonstrated, then it should be much easier in a human subject with bigger and wider blood vessels. However, feasibility is one thing, safety and efficacy is something else altogether and there was surely a long way to go before anyone could even consider attempting to treat an actual human patient. I was totally unaware that Parodi had already jumped the gun, and Volodos before him.

Fortune, they say, favours the brave. This one operation secured for Parodi, fame and fortune, in spades. But he had been very lucky. The aneurysm remained intact, unruptured long enough for the patient to die from other causes but, in actual fact, the operation he had performed was, technically, a failure. Based upon the rudimentary information gained from animal experiments, the device he used, consisted of a tube of Dacron fabric with a metal stent stitched to the top end to hold it in place. The bottom end, was left, just hanging free, without a stent; and there was nothing to stop blood filling back into, and pressurising the aneurysm. It was just a matter of good fortune that it did not rupture prior to the patient's death from other causes.

However, Parodi had demonstrated beyond doubt, the feasibility of introducing an endovascular graft into a human aorta without major surgery and this opened the floodgates for others to attempt the same thing.

It would be another four years, before the first commercial aortic endograft was available. If we had had access to a suitable stent, we could have constructed makeshift devices of our own in Liverpool. But there were no stents licensed for this use at the time, and manufacturers would not accept liability for any adverse outcomes. They were being released to a very small number of selected research units only and we were not one.

The critical issue was that minimally invasive treatment of aortic aneurysms as a whole was a totally unproven concept. Parodi got away with the first operation that failed, but treatment of patients with an otherwise fatal disease is not something that can be subjected to chance. Beyond demonstrating the technical feasibility of delivering an endograft into an aorta, there was no animal model possible for assessment of safety or efficacy, so humans were the only valid testbed.

The first, commercially available, aortic endograft was developed by a French vascular surgeon called Claude Mialhe. Having visited Parodi in Argentina, he realised that, in order for an endograft to work, it would have to have a stent at the bottom end as well as at the top. He also noted that the aneurysm usually extended all the way to the bottom end of the aorta; and that to seal it off effectively, would require an endograft with two legs, like a pair of trousers, to fit into the two main branches. He designed an ingenious system that involved construction of a bifurcated endograft from components that were assembled inside the patient under X-ray guidance. He worked in the town of Draguignan in the south of France and his device, which was given the name Stentor, was manufactured by a small Company, called Mintec, in La Ciotat near to Marseille. I was introduced to Claude Mialhe by my friend and colleague from the European Board of Vascular Surgery, the Dutchman Jaap Buth, and I invited him to Liverpool to demonstrate his Endograft. We selected patients who we thought were most suitable and who, after having been informed explicitly of the risks as well as the potential benefits, were willing to be treated with an 'experimental' device.

I liked Claude and learned a lot from him but he was not so well-appreciated by everyone and especially not by the vascular surgical establishment in France. A couple of years after first meeting him, I found myself defending him against a vicious professional assassination attempt.

The vascular surgical *capo di tutti capi* in France at the time, was a man by the name of Edouard Kieffer, who worked at the *Hôpital de la Pitié-Salpêtrière* in Paris. A portly *bon viveur,* he had great charisma which, allied to a distinctly Napoleonic autocratic tendency, gave him great influence over all the happenings in the sphere of vascular surgery throughout the French speaking world. He was the leading force behind the *Société Vasculaire de la Langue Francaise (SVLF),* and he had many followers including a surgeon from Marseille called Alain Branchereau who was effectively his 'right-hand-man'. Keiffer was a fast and technically brilliant surgeon of the old-school. His was one of the first vascular surgical units in Europe to amass a large series of thoracoabdominal total aortic replacement operations and it was largely due to him that vascular surgery was recognised as a speciality, separate from that of general surgery in France, long before the UK had followed suit.

I had met Edouard at a number of European vascular surgical gatherings in the 80s and, like many, was impressed with his style and the aura surrounding him. Invariably, the centre of attention, he was an engaging raconteur, equally accomplished in English as in French, and with a vast selection of humorous stories. However, some time before the Claude Mialhe fiasco erupted, I had encountered another side to his character. In my forays into Europe as representative of the Vascular Surgical Society, I had become well-acquainted with my counterpart in the SVLF a man by the name of called Jean-Pierre Becquemin. Finding that we had much in common, and in the interests of Anglo-French friendship, we agreed that one of his trainees, a young man named Pascal Desgranges, would come to work with me in Liverpool for six months. The idea was to broaden his experience of vascular surgery and the English language. Pascal fitted in extremely well in Liverpool. He was a good team member and a passionate supporter of Liverpool football club. He developed a curious blend of French and Scouse accents that doubtfully improved his powers of communication in English, much beyond the immediate vicinity of Liverpool. But, this apart, his visit was a great success. However, when I was invited to give a paper at a meeting of the French Language Vascular Society subsequently, I was surprised to find Jean-Pierre turning up with a lawyer. Edouard Kieffer, for whatever reason, had taken exception to him and decided his term as SVLF Secretary General would be terminated prematurely. One of the issues was the visit of Pascal Desgranges to Liverpool, which it was claimed had been paid for, inappropriately from SVLF funds. Not only did Jean-Pierre survive the opprobrium of Edouard Kieffer unscathed, he went on to eclipse him as the undisputed leader of French vascular surgery in the years that followed.

Claude Mialhe was not a part of the French vascular surgical establishment, working as he did, out in the 'sticks', and was certainly not a favoured member of the Edouard Kieffer inner circle. However, as inventor of the first commercial aortic endograft, he soon accumulated a large experience of endovascular aneurysm operations and his papers began to attract attention around the world, not least in America where the Food and Drugs Administration (FDA) was effectively stifling the clinical development of endovascular aneurysm repair on that side of the Atlantic. It did not help Claude, at all, that he enjoyed a close friendship with Jean-Pierre Becquemin. To the Parisian surgical elite in the grand teaching hospitals of the capital city, Draguignan was the epitome of the uncultured provincial south and could not possibly be the source of anything remotely edifying. Initially, Claude was simply ignored and then ridiculed for the notion that an aortic aneurysm could be treated by any means other than a 'proper' operation. But, when others started to take notice, something had to be done. At around this time, I chanced upon Edouard Kieffer and Alain Branchereau in a bar at a meeting somewhere in France. They went out of their way to inform me that Claude Mialhe was a crook. That he had fabricated his results. "For my own good," they told me, "I should have nothing more to do with him."

I had no doubts about Claude Mialhe's integrity but his data, at this time, did no more than confirm the feasibility of the procedure itself. They told us nothing about how effective the treatment was in terms of preventing patients dying from ruptured aneurysms or the risk of later complications. No one, Claude included, was any wiser as to what would happen in the long run and, in this respect, there were serious concerns that needed to be addressed urgently. What is more the royalties that Claude received from the sale of his Stentor devices, undoubtedly, undermined his personal credibility in some eyes. What was needed was independent analysis of the results of endovascular aneurysm repair over an extended period of time. And, sufficient data for reliable statistical analysis to be accrued in the shortest possible time.

In April 1995, I convened a meeting in Liverpool to which colleagues from Europe and Scandinavia with like-minded interest to determine the validity of minimally invasive endovascular repair for treatment of aortic aneurysms were invited. At this meeting, it was agreed to set up a European-wide Registry, which we labelled EUROSTAR, an anachronism for the European Registry of Stent graft techniques for Aortic Aneurysm Repair. Jaap Buth secured facilities for collation and analysis of the data at his hospital in Eindhoven and Claude Mialhe agreed to hand over the records of all of the patients, he had treated to date, in order to get the registry started.

A short time after this, Claude was summoned before the French equivalent of General Medical Council at the instigation of Edouard Kieffer, accused of malpractice and falsifying data. He was fully acquitted with support from the EUROSTAR organisation.

The first problem for the EUROSTAR group was that of funding. Jaap had access to space and some basic facilities in Eindhoven, but if the project was to succeed, we would need someone to do the work and for that we needed to raise money to pay a salary. In the absence of charitable or government grant monies, our only option was to approach commercial companies for funding. Aware, that dependence upon a single company would raise suspicions of bias and undermine the credibility of our registry data, we came up with a plan to raise money from multiple providers of aortic endografts in an even-handed way. By this time, several companies were investing in the new technology. All were based in the USA. They had registries of their own as essential tools for continuing development of their own technologies but the data, they published, was regarded with considerable suspicion of commercial bias. We reasoned, as it turns out correctly, that they would welcome independent analysis of performance data relating to their products and we came up with a deal whereby, in return for financial support, we would make available to them, two independently analysed sets of data; the first relating to their devices alone and the second, the aggregated data on all the devices together. It was an imperfect but pragmatic approach designed to eliminate actual or perceived bias in favour of any one Company.

Following its launch in 1996, the EUROSTAR Project was an instant success. By this time, interest in endovascular aneurysm repair was intense and nearly everybody wanted to be involved. But everyone shared the same serious ethical dilemma associated with treating a fatal disease with a new technique for which, there was so far, no supporting evidence. Nobody knew whether it would be effective in preventing rupture of aneurysms in the long term. After all, in contrast to conventional surgery, the aneurysm remained *in-situ* in the body and there were justifiable concerns that an endograft inner tube may not protect it from rupture, indefinitely. The EUROSTAR Registry offered a way out of this dilemma. Anxiety was mitigated by contributing to a much-needed scientific study to establish evidence, either way, in the shortest possible time. We soon had data for analysis on thousands of patients from all parts of the European Continent and Scandinavia.

It would be an understatement to say that the initial results were unpropitious. They were disastrous! They could have brought the entire concept to an abrupt end! We knew already, that the operative procedure itself, was safe and this was confirmed, but we were interested in what happened after that. To our horror, what happened after that was that the endografts disintegrated inside the body. The first results related to Claude Mialhe's original Stentor endografts, virtually all of which had had to be removed within the space of a couple of years. Patients in whom disintegration of the endograft was not detected remained at risk of death from rupture; a fate that, sadly, was visited upon quite a number. It was clear that this device had not been engineered to withstand the repetitive forces it would encounter inside the human aorta. Subjected to upwards of 36 million pulses a year, the struts of the metal stents fractured and the fabric wore away, leaving holes through which the blood escaped to refill the aneurysm. It was nothing short of calamitous. Aneurysms continued to rupture and when disintegration of the device was recognised by X-ray surveillance, before this happened, open surgery to remove and replace it with a sutured Dacron graft was considerably more difficult, and dangerous, than a normal conventional operation. As a consequence, whatever happened, the mortality rate was frighteningly high. In other words, far from improving the chances of surviving an aneurysm, endovascular repair with this device, at least, worsened them considerably.

That could have been the end of the story, was it not for the fact that the technology was evolving very rapidly with creation of new and better designs of endograft and EUROSTAR was uniquely placed to contribute data to inform this process of evolution. Within a very short time, we had sufficient data, not only to provide reliable information on outcomes overall, but also for detailed analysis of the modes, or reasons, for failure of the devices; vital information to guide future development of the technology. By the time the Stentor story was fully apparent, Mintec, which manufactured it, had been bought out by Boston Scientific, a large medical devices manufacturer, in the USA and they set about re-engineering it. The basic design was preserved but stronger and more robust materials were used in its construction. It was renamed Vanguard.

The early Vanguard results were much better than those of Stentor. Metal strut fractures and fabric holes were a rarity and it seemed that the problems had been resolved. Consequently, the Boston Scientific Vanguard device quickly became established as the worldwide market leader. However, after a time, there were reports of aneurysms rupturing after treatment with Vanguard endografts and anxiety about the safety and efficacy of this device also began to resurface. Everyone knew that EUROSTAR was in possession of a large database and we found ourselves at the centre of a growing controversy. Led by Robert Rutherford, Professor at the University of Colorado and an eminent and highly respected doyenne of vascular surgery in the States, we came under intense pressure for immediate disclosure of our data on Vanguard. We had been watching a trend in the figures that, if confirmed statistically, would indicate it to be an unsafe device. In accordance with the contractual arrangements we had with all companies who subscribed to EUROSTAR, we had been obliged to make the data available to

Boston Scientific first and our contacts in the company were becoming increasingly nervous. They had made an enormous investment in the Vanguard project and, if it was to fail, the financial consequences for the company would be catastrophic. We had a number of meetings during which they offered various explanations for what was happening, focussing on issues such as surgeons' selection of patients for treatment, which they indicated would account for failure if inappropriate, or the methodology for collection and analysis of the data. There were certainly high stakes involved for Boston Scientific but we were more concerned about the implications and consequences for the many thousands of patients around the world who had had Vanguard devices implanted. Accordingly, we agreed internally that we would not disclose any data publicly until we were certain of the facts, in other words until we had incontrovertible statistical evidence of device failure.

The weather in Phoenix, Arizona in February is invariably beautiful. Blue skies, clear dry desert air and temperatures in the upper 20s were the backdrop to the Annual Congress of the International Society for Endovascular Specialists (ISES) organised for many years by a colourful character called Ted Diethrich. Ted was a pioneer of endovascular therapies and a great showman. He died in 2017 from a brain tumour, almost certainly, caused by exposure to excessive radiation incurred during the course of many endovascular surgical procedures he had performed over a long period of time. Surgeons from all parts of the United States and around the world, especially those with less benign winter weather, flocked to Phoenix every year in thousands to join in his jamboree. The programme was a mixture of 'live' cases projected on enormous screens and scientific presentations on research projects and clinical trials. In the late 90s and early 2000s, there was considerable interest in the EUROSTAR data at these meetings and, for a time, I was UK representative on the ISES Council. It was at one of these events, that I first presented our results on the Vanguard device. Statistical analysis of the data, in the week before, had finally disclosed results that were unequivocally statistically significant. Within five years of treatment, one out of every ten patients with a Vanguard device, had suffered rupture of their aneurysm, often with fatal consequences. These data could not be explained away on the basis of inappropriate patient selection. It was very doubtful that treatment of an aneurysm with a Vanguard device improved at all upon the natural history of the disease or the chances of the patient living a longer life.

The conference hall was packed and sitting amongst the audience was a large delegation of senior Boston Scientific executives and scientists. They were furious. After my presentation they descended upon me to vent their anger. They had not been given access to a script of the presentation beforehand, for which some criticism was perhaps justified, but they had no answer to the fundamental issue, that the Vanguard device was not an effective treatment for aortic aneurysms. There was none.

The primary cause of failure of the Vanguard device was that it slipped. Pressure exerted by the spring-like 'sealing' stent, against the wall of the aorta above the aneurysm, was insufficient to hold it in place in the flowing, pulsating blood stream and when it moved the 'seal' was broken and blood leaked around it to refill the aneurysm sac. Other endovascular aortic graft manufacturers had fitted hooks or barbs to the stent to prevent this type of slippage and it might have been an option for Boston Scientific engineers to incorporate this change, but it was too late, the damage was done. The clinical community had lost confidence in Vanguard and a month or two later, it was withdrawn from the market permanently. Boston Scientific never entered the aortic endograft market again.

That, so many prosthetic endografts, had been implanted into the bodies of so many patients, with such disastrous consequences, should have been an international scandal, especially in Europe and Australasia, where most had taken place. The Vanguard and the Stentor device, before it, had serious technical flaws that should have been predicted by preclinical laboratory stress testing, before being released for implantation in patients. In the United States, the regulatory authority, The Federal Drugs Administration (FDA), had severely restricted the use of these devices to a very small number of specially licensed medical centres under very specific research conditions. In effect, the absence of an effective regulation system for evaluation of new prosthetic devices in Europe was the reason for the success of EUROSTAR. It had fulfilled an essential need. The disclosure in Phoenix, increased awareness, and I was interviewed for an article in the USA Today newspaper expressing concern about the safety of aortic endografts.

Subsequently, I was contacted for advice by the UK Medical and Healthcare Regulatory Authority (MHRC) which is linked to the European Regulatory Authority but regulation in Europe remained very light, compared to that exercised by the FDA.

The EUROSTAR project lasted ten years, at the end of which, most of the technical problems associated with minimally invasive endovascular repair of aortic aneurysms had been ironed out. The programme was terminated in 2006. However, the big question that EUROSTAR was unable to answer was whether this new approach was better for patients in the long run than conventional open surgery. This was the subject of another landmark research study with which, I was also very much involved.

In 1998, a notice appeared in the British Medical Journal inviting applications for an NHS HTA (Health Technologies Assessment) grant to undertake a national clinical trial of endovascular aneurysm repair. Evidence-based medicine was the new mantra and NICE, the National Institute for Clinical Excellence, later to be renamed the National Institute for Health and Care Excellence, was about to be launched by the Department of Health. Aortic endografts were extremely expensive and the initial cost to the NHS of endovascular aneurysm repair was significantly higher than that of conventional open surgery. It was being paid for in some centres in the UK, Liverpool included, despite there being no clear evidence of clinical or cost benefit over the pre-existing standard of open surgery. The powers-that-be decided, not unreasonably, that significant evidence of superiority was needed before it could be rolled out for routine use in all NHS hospitals. My colleagues and I in Liverpool agreed and we prepared a grant application for submission to the NHS HTA.

To be the recipient of a multi-million-pound research grant is a big feather in the cap for the academically ambitious. At the same time the grant giver takes a risk by entrusting millions of pounds of public or charitable funds to one individual or organisation. Two principal determinants of where research monies go are, track record and networking. This opens up significant possibilities for collusion between established givers and receivers of research grants; a convenient arrangement which is perpetuated by the fact that regular recipients, frequently ascend onto the boards of donors. In the fullness of time, those who play the system well, stand a good chance of a knighthood. It is a system that is difficult for the outsider to break into. Up in Liverpool, we were blissfully unaware of these wheels within wheels. Down in London, there was someone who knew exactly how the system worked and who lacked, neither the ambition nor the guile, necessary to benefit. It was my old friend, Roger Greenhalgh.

Naively believing our proposals met all of the requirements set out in the NHS HTA invitation for bids, we thought we were in with a good chance. And then, I got a call from Roger. Having just led a national trial to determine how best to manage patients with small aneurysms, for which he garnered most of the accolades, this new trial represented his next big opportunity. He must have had access to inside information about applications submitted by other centres because we were all invited to a meeting at Charing Cross Hospital. There he proposed that, rather than compete with each other for the grant money, we should all get together to prepare a single joint application. On the face of it, this seemed like a very sensible idea.

First, we would have to agree upon the structure and objectives of the joint trial proposal. This was not straightforward because there were two completely different ideas on the table. One from Liverpool that proposed to compare endovascular and conventional open repair in a population of patients who were deemed suitable for either option; and the other from Charing Cross that proposed to study only those patients who were considered too frail or ill, as a consequence of coexisting heart or lung disease, to withstand the trauma of conventional open surgery. Patients in the Charing Cross trial would be randomly allocated, either to be treated by endovascular repair of their aneurysm or to have no interventional treatment of any sort. It was decided at this first meeting that both trials had merit and that they would both would be offered to the NHS within a single joint application. The Liverpool proposal would be designated Endovascular Aneurysm Repair trial 1 (EVAR 1) and the Charing Cross proposal EVAR 2. It was agreed that Roger would prepare the application for submission on everyone's behalf.

Given my previous encounters with Roger, it should have come as no surprise to me to find Charing Cross/Imperial College designated as the sole applicant when details of the successful submission became known. Roger's disingenuity, it seemed, knew no bounds. He maintained that it had never been his intention to submit a joint application involving another centre but, up in Liverpool, we were incensed. We had not even been accorded a representative on the proposed trial management committee. In response to our protests, I was invited, belatedly, to join the trial management committee as a representative of the EUROSTAR Registry. Liverpool was not accorded any merit or share of the funding, which over the entire course of the trial, amounted to several million pounds.

Of the vascular centres involved in the EVAR trials throughout the UK, Liverpool and Newcastle were the biggest contributors of data. Charing Cross contributed relatively few patients. In the event, EVAR 2 was heavily criticised for its design and the results largely discounted. EVAR 1 had considerably more impact, but the results of this trial were not entirely conclusive either. Unsurprisingly, the minimally invasive procedure was safer in the short term but ten years later, the overall death rate was lower in the open surgery group. None of this really mattered much though, because, by the time the definitive results were known, on-going technological advances, improving clinical expertise and patient preference had established EVAR firmly as the treatment of choice worldwide. I stuck with the EVAR Trial Management Committee for a year or two, following publication of the early results in the Lancet and other journals. However, when it transpired that Roger was planning to sell trial data to a US endograft manufacturer in support of an application for approval of their aortic endograft by the Food and Drugs Administration (FDA) in order to fund more research at Imperial College, I decided, enough was enough and resigned. Faced with overwhelming criticism from other quarters also, Roger was obliged to find his money from another source. It did not take him long.

Technological advances underpinning endovascular aneurysm repair progressed rapidly in the 2000s. Initially, the procedure was applicable only to those patients with the simplest, uncomplicated aneurysms. However, one innovation in particular, made it possible to treat many more patients including those with complex thoracoabdominal aortic diseases. This was the incorporation of branches. In Australia, mainly in Adelaide and Perth, surgeons working with the American Company, Cook, first came up with the idea of making fenestrations, or holes, in the fabric of the endograft to enable blood to flow through them into side branches of the aorta. Previously, the necessity to avoid blocking off vital branches, particularly those to the kidneys, meant that only patients with aneurysms arising below these arteries could be treated. Fenestrations that allowed blood to flow through into the kidney arteries permitted treatment of aneurysms that were very close to, or above, these branches to be treated. It worked, but a serious issue was that every patient's anatomy is unique and consequently, fenestrations had to be individually tailor-made and this was a long and very expensive process.

Tim Chuter, who was now established as Professor in San Francisco, came up with an alternative approach. He developed aortic endografts with branches incorporated into them. They were short and had to be connected into the natural branches, by additional stents, inside the patient under X-ray guidance. However, they did not have to be bespoke, and were immediately available 'off-the-shelf'. The operative procedures involved in deploying branched endografts are challenging and demand a very high level of technical skill but they can be a life-saving alternative to major surgery for some patients. Julian Brooks was one such.

Tim Chuter had just started to experiment with prototype branched endografts in 1998, when Abbas and I first operated upon Julian to replace his aorta. Endovascular thoraco-abdominal aneurysm repair was definitely not a practical option at that time. Four years later, it was still highly experimental, mostly being undertaken by Tim himself. I first met him at a small brainstorming event in Australia sponsored by Cook. At the time, he was working on his first prototypes. He was a keen marathon runner and we went jogging together along a riverbank between sessions. Subsequently, we would meet up regularly at vascular congresses around the world and go running together.

Having come up against an apparent surgical impasse with Julian, it occurred to me, albeit without great expectations, that minimally invasive endovascular treatment of his life-threatening situation might just be possible. So, we sent copies of the X-ray images to Tim. The aberrant anatomy with duplicated arteries to the liver meant that it would be even more complex than usual, necessitating a unique configuration of branches. Tim was up for it and, three months later, he arrived in Liverpool with a custom-built branched aortic endograft.

The procedure itself was not quick. It took the best part of eight hours to complete but at the finish, Julian's ballooned 'time-bomb' aortic patch had been defused by exclusion from the circulation and all vital organs remained perfused with blood. What had seemed impossible, just a few months previously, had been achieved without major surgery and without risk of massive haemorrhage. Julian recovered fully within hours and left the hospital, after just a couple of days. Compared to what he had endured before, it seemed like nothing short of a miracle.

Chapter 9
John and Stuart

It was a warmer than average evening, for the time of the year, on Monday, 1ˢᵗ May 1995. A VW Passat was heading west, down North Hill Street from Toxteth, towards The Dingle, south of Liverpool City centre. The Bank holiday traffic, was light but there was nothing remarkable about the scene otherwise. Then suddenly, out of nowhere, a black VW Golf screeched to a halt in front of the Passat, blocking its path and a masked man jumped out brandishing an automatic weapon. The driver of the Passat scrambled out of the car and ran for his life, but the gunman opened fire mowing him down. Bystanders looked on in fear and horror, as the killer drove off at speed, leaving his victim bleeding to death on the road.

The subject of this gangland execution was a well-known Liverpool 'businessman' with the unusual name of David Ungi. He was 35 years of age and the head of a large Toxteth dynasty. In their patch, the Ungi family was nobility and treated with great deference and respect. His funeral at Our Lady of Mount Carmel Catholic Church on High Park Street was an occasion, befitting one of his status. A hundred and fifty family members and friends were conveyed to the church in 31 stretch limos that took five minutes to pass. It was November and their Marbella tans and gold jewellery contrasted with the pallid drabness of the large crowd assembled on the road outside. A lorry float followed the limos covered in flowers, floral tributes to 'Dad', 'Uncle', 'Brother' and 'Gent' and a five-feet high tableau depicting his picture and a dove.

No one was ever brought to justice for the murder. The police knew who the perpetrators were but securing hard evidence, was another matter. The bystanders were afraid to talk and the Ungi family themselves preferred to deal with the matter in their own way. A vendetta followed, that saw 22 shootings in ten days, and armed police patrolling the streets of a UK city for the first time in peacetime. A year later, there were rumours that two men presumed to be responsible for the killing had been shot dead in Jamaica.

There was a lucrative trade in drugs in Liverpool in the 90s. 'Black' crack, cocaine, heroin, amphetamines, cannabis and Ecstasy were all readily available. Despite some evidence of recovery from the social problems that led to the riots of 1981, there were still high levels of unemployment, especially among the young and they were targeted primarily. With a prevailing sense of abandonment and hopelessness, they were particularly vulnerable and some turned to crime to fund their habits.

Given the status and deference afforded to those at the top of the drug dealing hierarchy, and their opulent riches, it is not surprising, that there were youths who aspired to emulate them. Drug barons and top footballers were Liverpool's 'royalty'. It was probably easy enough to get onto the lower rungs as 'runners' or street dealers but woe betide those who imagined they could 'go it alone'. Chances were, they would be punished with a shot in an arm or a leg, or even killed. The drug barons themselves had a perilous existence as turf wars led to sporadic outbreaks of 'tit for tat' shootings. Gradually, drug dealing spread out from the city centre into the suburbs, eventually, coming close to home, in our case, literally.

One day, high fences, impenetrable automatic gates and sophisticated CCTV surveillance were installed at a house, a few doors down from ours on the opposite side of the road. Ostensibly, a second-hand car dealer; we were reliably informed that the new owner was a well-known drug baron. I saw him only once. One morning in early summer, I returned home from an emergency at the hospital in the small hours. It was about 4.00 am and the sun was just rising. Through the window, I saw our near neighbour walking down the middle of the road with his dog on a lead and his 'minders' walking along level with him on each side of the road. Someone had had a shot at him in his driveway previously and he was leaving nothing to chance. Given the extraordinary measures he had to take just to stay alive it did not seem to me to be a very enviable life-style but, far from being deterred, young thugs thought it glamorous.

Everyone knew what he was up to but it took years for the police to gather sufficient evidence to bring him to justice. Eventually, he was locked up and all his possessions, his house included, were confiscated in a highly publicised raid that was shown live on BBC News as a warning to other 'wannabe' drug barons.

In the midst of a flare up of 'tit-for-tat' shootings that followed the killing of David Ungi, a good-looking man in his 30s, let's call him John, was leaving his gym at the Pier Head in the city centre. He paused at the door and surveyed the car park. Seeing nothing unusual, he unlocked his top-of-the-range BMW with the remote fob before walking quickly to it across the open space. Just as he was opening the rear door to throw the holdall containing his sports gear onto the back seat, he became aware of a car driving along the exit lane of the car park with two men inside and turned for a better look. At that moment, the car jerked to a stop in front of him and the man in the passenger seat leaped out with a sawn-off shotgun in his hand. There was no possibility of escape. The gun was discharged with a loud explosion and, as his assailants roared-off with screeching tyres, John fell to the floor, blood pouring from his left groin.

I was on a ward round at The Royal, when I got an urgent call from A&E. There were blue lights and armed police everywhere. John was on a trolley in 'Majors' and there was lots of blood. He was very pale but fully conscious and remarkably calm. Most of the shots had penetrated his thigh and the amount of bleeding and massive swelling of his thigh suggested injury to the femoral artery. It had apparently not been the intention of the gunman to kill but to maim and it was a good attempt because the leg was at serious risk. X-ray pictures showed a dense collection of lead shot in the upper thigh, beneath the patch of severely peppered skin. Despite obvious injury to the femoral artery, the major nerves close by seemed to be intact because he could move his leg and had no loss of sensation. But there was massive internal bleeding from the traumatised femoral artery and absent pulses signalled that the circulation to the lower leg had been compromised.

In the operating theatre, we found the upper end of the femoral artery was shredded beyond repair and would have to be replaced. There was an enormous collection of blood in the thigh and the muscles were suffused with blood and extremely swollen. The femoral vein alongside the artery was also destroyed. In contrast to arteries there is plenty of spare capacity in the venous system and we just tied it off to stop the bleeding from it. Fortunately for him, the saphenous vein on the inner side of the thigh had not been damaged and was available to be used for construction of a graft to replace the damaged femoral artery. We picked out with forceps all the lead shot we could see but there were plenty left behind buried within the muscles that would stay there forever. John was fit and strong and easily able to withstand the blood loss and the trauma of surgery. A couple of hours later, he was fully awake again and ready to be transferred from the recovery unit to the ward, where he occupied a private room. Two police officers sat outside the door wearing bullet-proof vests and cradling Heckler & Koch MP5 sub-machine guns in their laps. It was not unknown for further attacks on victims to be made in hospital.

John spent two weeks recuperating in this room. Clean cut, handsome, personable and intelligent, he was relaxed, cheerful and apparently unphased by the brutal attack inflicted upon him. He was the quintessential enterprising successful businessman. His girlfriend, on the other hand, was a typical gangster's moll. Petite and pretty, she clip-clopped down the hospital corridor daily in improbably high-heeled shoes and the sort of miniskirt that had long been out of fashion but which showed off to perfection, a pair of very shapely legs. She did not speak to anyone other than John. His mother, on the other hand, also a regular visitor, had quite a lot to say. A typical Scouse matriarch, she doted upon him and went out of her way to impress upon everyone, what a good boy her John was and how he was an "innocent victim of criminal scum." John's only other regular visitors, were the police. Unsurprisingly, given the constant police presence, his male friends stayed away. The detectives, seemingly, got no useful information out of him. John, who certainly knew who his assailants were, was saying nothing. One day, one of the detectives intimated to me that I should let him know if, by chance, John should let slip any information that might be of interest. This did not seem to me to be an entirely proper proposition to put to a doctor who is bound to respect professional confidentiality although, in truth, I was more concerned about my own welfare as a source of incriminating information. Out of curiosity, I did ask John if he knew who had shot him. He merely smiled enigmatically in response. It was better for me not to know.

John was far too smart to be taking drugs himself. But, while he was making an assured recovery and joshing with the nurses in his comfortable guarded room, another man of about the same age was lying in agony, in a bed elsewhere in the hospital. The two men did not know each other but they were both dependent upon illegal drugs; one to fund a lavish expensive lifestyle and the other for the fixes that made his miserable life bearable from one day to the next. It was rare for there not to be at least one drug addict patient under the care of the vascular service at any one time. Stuart was typical and nearing the end of a long and miserable journey.

I did not know much about him. When admitted, he was already in a poor physical and mental state, but in his more lucid moments, he seemed intelligent and well-educated. According to his medical records, he had been married and had children, but no one ever visited him. A confirmed heroin addict, he was well-known to the staff at Drug Addiction Centre in Roscoe Street and they advised us on the dose of Methadone to administer to him in place of heroin while he was in hospital. When he first presented in the A&E Department, there was an enormous abscess discharging copious foul-smelling pus from his left groin and most of the left leg was already decayed beyond redemption. He was close to death with infection raging throughout his body.

His was a common story. When addicts first start injecting heroin, they use veins in their arms. When these become blocked as a result of repeated punctures, with none-too-clean needles, they move to other places where there are other accessible veins and eventually, end up in the groins. Here, the femoral vein, which lies along the inner side of the femoral artery just beneath the skin makes a large and easily accessible target. Although, it cannot be seen, the pulse in the artery is easy to feel and a good guide for the needle puncture. The intention is to inject into the vein, to start with at least; but despite its large size, it also becomes blocked sooner or later by blood clots and scar tissue. As a last resort, Stuart, like many before him, had resorted to injecting into the femoral artery itself. When this stage is reached, it is only a matter of time before blood-leaking back out of the artery into the surrounding fat becomes infected to form an abscess. Infected clots carried down the leg in the blood stream then form multiple other abscesses. This was the situation presented by Stuart on arrival. There was never any chance of saving his lower leg and the issue was, at what level would we have to amputate for there to be a reasonable chance of the stump healing. An X-ray of the arteries showed that the main femoral artery no longer existed. Some blood was getting into the thigh through small alternative channels but doubtfully sufficient to sustain healing at any level and I decided, therefore, that we would have to attempt some sort of reconstruction of the artery.

In the operating theatre, we started by excising devitalised skin overlying the huge abscess in the groin. There was, at least, a pint of pungent green pus mixed with infected blood clots. Dense scar tissue made for slow and difficult dissection but eventually we found a small artery deep below the groin which we were able to connect to the iliac artery above the groin with a short vein graft. We then, set about amputating the leg high in the upper thigh. We cut away devitalised infected muscle and sawed through the femur, just below the hip joint. Rather than close the wound with stitches we packed it with swabs soaked in an antiseptic so that infection was not trapped inside.

Stuart's general condition did improve for a time afterwards and there were some signs that the stump was starting to heal. About a week after the operation, he was well enough to be transferred out of intensive care and back to the ward but a day or two later, disaster struck. I had a call to go urgently to the ward where there was a serious emergency. When I arrived the house officer was kneeling on Stuart's bed pressing hard on his groin. There was blood everywhere. Stuart's face was white and he was barely conscious. I knew, at once, that the vein graft had ruptured. Vein grafts, which have a high resistance to infection, occasionally succumb to it under extreme circumstances and this was a case in point. We could not just stand while he exsanguinated into the bed. So, we rushed him back to theatre. We did the only thing possible and that was to tie off completely all of the blood supply to the limb. After this, he lingered on for another three weeks in intensive care. All the remaining muscles in the stump died and started to liquify and the skin turned black. He developed a large pressure sore over his bottom which leaked copious pus also. I thought about a hindquarter amputation, which would have left him with no stump at all but decided there was little chance that this would heal either. In any case, despite massive doses of antibiotics, he remained severely infected and was requiring increasing amounts of adrenalin, noradrenalin and other chemical stimulants to keep his heart and circulation going. He would not have made it off the operating table. He died from septicaemic shock with no family members present, and apparently friendless.

I treated many young men and women addicts with similar catastrophic self-inflicted vascular injuries at that time and the situation is no different in hospitals today. Given that nothing has changed over the years it is evident that the policy of prohibition, is not working. It serves to make a small number of unscrupulous people, like John, very rich while doing nothing to protect the addicts. If we do not learn the lessons of the past, we are destined to go on making the same mistakes again while young people continue to die. In these circumstances, surely legalisation of drugs is worth a try. This would deprive dealers and drug barons of their lucrative business trading in human misery. and reduce the petty crime committed by users desperate for their next fix. Legalisation would not be to condone drug taking; quite the reverse. Tobacco consumption has declined dramatically as a consequence of campaigns that made it socially unacceptable. Even if the prevalence of drug taking is not reduced bringing it out of the shadows would ensure that addicts could be better supported and the process made safer with pharmaceutically standardised drugs and clean needles. Legalisation would require international cooperation and strong border controls but the effects could be hardly less disastrous than those of the failed policies of prohibition that have been tried so far.

Chapter 10
The leaving of Liverpool

"All new therapies work miraculously … for a while," is an axiom first attributed to a physician named Dr Eberden as long ago as 1805. And, for a while, when the first aortic endografts were falling apart inside patients' bodies, it seemed likely that endovascular treatment of aortic aneurysms might turn out to be little more than a 'one-day' wonder. However, major high-risk open operations were being superseded in all branches of surgery by minimally invasive interventions and there were few more major or higher-risk operations than those undertaken previously for aortic aneurysms. Endovascular repair was, therefore, an idea that took hold. The EUROSTAR Registry had sufficient data not only to identify problems at an early stage but also to analyse the causes of those problems and point the way to solutions. By 2006, the project had been running for ten years and had data on over 12,000 patients. It had made an important contribution to the evolution of the technology, which it now seemed clear, was here to stay. Not surprisingly, the incentive for contributors to maintain voluntarily the additional bureaucratic burden of submitting data to EUROSTAR diminished and the flow of information began to dry up. The programme had run its course and we decided to wind it up. Not that all controversies had been resolved, far from it. The initial results of UK EVAR randomised trials had been equivocal and there were legitimate, on-going concerns about the longer-term effects but there was confidence that as new issues arose new solutions would be found. There would be no going back.

Enthused by Tim Chuter and others, most noticeably Michael Lawrence-Brown in Western Australia and Roy Greenberg in Cleveland USA, we became increasingly engaged in treating aneurysms of ever-increasing complexity and challenging anatomy in Liverpool. As a result, patients were referred to us from all parts of the country. Our programme worked well because we had a talented team with the requisite disciplines of surgery and interventional radiology represented on an equal footing. Other units were not so lucky as territorial conflicts between surgeons and radiologists over image-guided endovascular treatments grumbled on.

In addition to the technical evolution of endovascular repair, the aortic aneurysm landscape was changing in other ways. In the dark ages of the 80s, when desperate attempts to save lives with big and bloody open operations at all hours of the day and night frequently ended in death and tears, the mortality rate from rupture of aortic aneurysms was in the order of 90 per cent. Sudden death at home or in the street, without any chance of life-saving surgery was the fate of the majority. Of those who did make it to the operating theatre, about half survived. Yet, if an aneurysm was diagnosed and operated upon before it ruptured, 95 per cent of the patients survived. The problem was that most aneurysms remained silent and, therefore, undiagnosed until the point of rupture. It was a situation that cried out for a screening test and the availability of ultrasound scanners made this a real possibility. A scan is cheap, easy, safe and a very effective diagnostic tool for aortic aneurysms. In 2002, Alan Scott, a surgeon working in Chichester on the south coast of England, published a paper in the British Journal of Surgery, on the results of a randomised trial to compare the death rate associated with aortic aneurysms in a population screened by ultrasound scans with that of an unscreened population. Those in whom an aneurysm was diagnosed by the scan were offered elective surgical treatment. The results of this trial were striking with a significantly lower aneurysm related death rate within five years in the screened population. This result led to submissions being made to the Department of Health to establish a nationwide aortic aneurysm-screening programme. In 2004, I was made President of the Vascular Society GB and Ireland and, in this role, became involved in this campaign. The Department of Health had a standing committee on screening programmes, the National Screening Committee (NSC) and I joined its Abdominal Aortic Aneurysm (AAA) Working Group as the Vascular Society representative. Given the unequivocal evidence of benefit in saving lives, it took a surprising amount of persuasion to win the day. One counter-argument was that AAA screening benefits elderly men who are no longer active in the workforce and, since they are a burden on the national economy, it would be considerably more cost-effective to let them die. A more cogent issue was that elective surgery itself carries an associated mortality risk and some patients, who had no symptoms at all, would die sooner rather than later as a direct consequence of screening. To be sure that deaths from surgery did not outweigh deaths from rupture, the operative mortality rate of screened patients would have to be extremely low. The case for AAA screening was finally accepted by the Department of Health with the one, essential, proviso that elective surgery on all screened patients would be confined to centres with an established track record of low operative mortality. The Vascular Society played a key role in ensuring that this was the case.

Following the instigation of the national AAA screening programme, the number of patients presenting with ruptured aortic aneurysms reduced considerably. And this coincided with significantly lower, operative mortality of elective treatment, associated with the wide adoption of minimally invasive endovascular repair.

Having brought the EUROSTAR Programme to a close, and with our own service in Liverpool, on a steady track, I started to think about my own future. I confess I was wearying of the NHS and its overbearing prescriptive bureaucracy. I was spending just as much time, or more, justifying what I was doing and arguing about money with individuals who had MBs in business studies and knew the cost of everything but the value of nothing. Deference to non-medical managers is accepted by most consultants in the NHS today but I had known a different time and found it hard to adjust. I had also lost enthusiasm for emergency calls in the middle of the night and at weekends. Accordingly, I decided to take a step back from the clinical front line and focus my energies on research.

A key player in the success of the Liverpool endovascular service was a gifted interventional radiologist and a truly excellent colleague by the name of Richard McWilliams. He had a flair for innovation from which the service profited greatly. I was pursuing a new idea with him that I hoped and believed would support a programme of research to keep me engaged in Liverpool for several years at least.

Having started at the lower end of the aorta, in the abdomen, with relatively simple endografts, we had worked our way progressively up into the chest and towards the heart and as we did so, the procedures became increasingly more complicated. The arch of the aorta which gives rise to the branches to the head was a particularly tricky challenge. The celebrated American heart surgeon, Denton Cooley, expressed this challenge well when he declared that, "The arch is the seat of the soul." Somehow, the arteries that supply all of the blood to the brain have to be connected to the endograft without interruption of the blood flow for more than a minute or two. Tim Chuter, amongst others, was experimenting with endografts incorporating branches, but the technical problems associated with locating and fixing these branches into the arteries to the brain were considerable.

Richard and I came up with another idea. It involved cutting a hole in the aortic endograft immediately after it had been deployed using a small instrument passed into the branch itself through a separate puncture in the skin of the neck. In theory, this technique would ensure that the hole matched the position of the natural branch exactly and a connecting stent entered along the same route as the cutting instrument would ensure they remained permanently aligned and connected. Essentially, a branched endograft would be constructed *in situ*. It had the potential advantage that it could be achieved using standard off-the-shelf components which would be much less expensive than a customised endograft with branches made to match the individual anatomy of the patient. We discussed the idea with Michael Lawrence-Brown in Western Australia. He had been the main instigator of fenestrated endografts that enabled the kidney arteries to be perfused when crossed by an endograft. This was a similar situation. We needed to see if it would work in an animal model first and Michael offered us access to his experimental facility in Perth. Given the almost impenetrable regulatory obstacles to animal experimentation in the UK, we gratefully accepted his offer. Richard travelled to Australia and undertook a number of successful procedures in dogs;

Shortly after Richard's return, we found our first willing patient. Our lady, let's call her Edith, had an 'ideal' aneurysm. It did not involve the main carotid arteries to the brain but it did involve the artery to the left arm, the subclavian artery, which came off the arch of the aorta close to the left carotid artery. Because the arm can tolerate prolonged interruption of its blood supply without disastrous consequences, Edith's aneurysm afforded the opportunity to try out our technique on the subclavian artery without risk to the brain. If it worked well in this situation there was a very good chance it would work just as well for the carotid arteries. It did indeed work well.

We decided we were on to something but in order to take the idea forward, we were going to need substantial financial support. A US medical device Company called, Medtronic, was interested. We submitted a research protocol with a five-year time-line to them and they agreed to support it to the tune of a million dollars. This was the chance, I had been looking for, to enable me step back from clinical practice while remaining closely connected with the Liverpool Unit I had built up.

With a firm offer from Medtronic under my belt, I set about disengaging myself from the clinical side of things. I relinquished my Clinical Directorship role in favour of John Brennan who had been with the unit for ten years and who I knew would do a good job. I then approached the General Manager for Surgery, a lady called Anne Doran, to propose a new clinical research contract for myself funded entirely by Medtronic. I explained that there would be no cost to the NHS but I would need access to NHS patients for trial purposes. It all seemed very reasonable and rational to me and I had not anticipated any problems. Unfortunately, Mrs Doran saw things differently. She told me that the Hospital Trust could not possibly accept the research monies from Medtronic, because to do so, might be seen to prejudice their procurement policies for endovascular aortic grafts. Despite my assurances to the contrary, she was adamant and when I appealed to the CEO I got the same answer. I then approached the University of Liverpool who would surely accept the Medtronic grant. They did, but only on the condition that the University would be the sole owner of all intellectual property resulting from the research. Unsurprisingly, this was not at all acceptable to Medtronic whose motives were entirely commercial and not in the least philanthropic. After several months trying to find a solution Medtronic withdrew their offer. Subsequently, the money went to a charming lady vascular surgeon from Istanbul who did an excellent good job of developing our idea.

Having divested myself of the clinical leadership role and with no appetite to continue on the NHS vascular surgery frontline as a foot soldier, I resigned from the Royal Liverpool University Hospital and, despite zero experience of sailing, I bought a sailing boat capable of crossing oceans. I called her 'Free Spirit'.

Chapter 11

University College London Hospital

The first sea breezes had hardly stirred the sails of my beautiful new boat, when I had a call, out of the blue, from a vascular surgeon at University College Hospital in London. Mo was not someone I knew well, but we had been contemporaries in the small world of vascular surgery for years. He told me, he was due to retire and they were looking for someone to replace him. Would I be interested? Given that we were the same age and that I had myself just retired, it seemed a strange proposition indeed. Any resemblance to the job I had just left, held no attraction for me whatsoever, but I was intrigued and I decided to pay University College Hospital a visit.

UCLH is an impressive, modern, tall, glass and steel structure, resplendent in white cladding, situated on the corner of Tottenham Court Road and Euston Road. Overlooking the old Victorian buildings on Gower Street it replaced, it was the showpiece hospital of the day; a jewel in the crown of the NHS. Just before my visit, it had acquired additional notoriety as the final residence of Alexander Litvinenko, the ex-KGB agent. Neither the first, nor the last traitor of Putin's Russia to suffer the ultimate retribution on English soil; he died in the intensive care unit from Polonium 210-induced radiation poisoning. Andy Webb, the Medical Director, himself an intensive care specialist, pointed out the room in which he died when showing me the facilities the hospital had to offer.

The UCLH vascular surgery service had not achieved the same heights, nationally or internationally, in recent years as neighbouring St Mary's, Charing Cross and The Royal Free Hospitals. Andy Webb fostered ambitions to raise its profile, as did the CEO, Sir Robert Naylor, apparently. I was to discover later, that this was not just a matter of pride but an issue of strategic significance in the highly competitive world of London teaching hospital politics. I knew nothing of this and had no inkling of shenanigans that were going on behind the scenes.

Andy confidently predicted that an upgrade of vascular surgery services would be backed up with serious money, if they had a credible development plan to work to. They were looking for someone to formulate and implement such a plan.

I was sufficiently interested to return to the hospital again to meet with and sound-out the existing team. On my side, I wanted to make clear that I was not looking for a return to front-line NHS clinical practice but would be interested to work with them to see what we could achieve, in terms of improving the profile of the hospital, if that is what they wanted. I assumed that the thinking behind the approach to me was that some of the assets underlying the success of the Liverpool endovascular programme might be transferable.

In addition to Mo Adiseshiah, who was about to leave, there were two other surgeons. Obi Agu, of Nigerian origin, was the younger one. Having been in post for a relatively short time, he was ambitiously striving to build a personal clinical practice in both the NHS and private sectors. The other, Chris Bishop, in his 50s was firmly established in Harley Street, or more precisely Devonshire Street. Chris was an enthusiastic supporter of the NHS, but did not have too much time to commit to it himself. He fulfilled the basics demanded by his contract, which was as basic as you could get in terms of enforceable obligations. He was one of a small number of consultants who had rejected the time-based contract brought in by the NHS, some years previously. In theory, at least, he was still an independent contractor. This did not cut much ice with the non-clinical managers who treated him much like anybody else but from his point of view he could pursue his extensive private interests without any sense of guilt. And, to be fair, unlike many with Harley Street practices, I never knew him to cheat on his commitments to the NHS, such as they were. Both Chris and Obi were very welcoming and seemed unreservedly enthusiastic about my possible involvement at UCLH.

I met only one interventional radiologist at this visit. His name was Joe Brookes. Although, he was also welcoming and apparently enthusiastic, he was about to start a two-year sabbatical in Barbados, supposedly working in the hospital in Bridgetown. He was not going to be around for this period of time. There were two younger radiologists who I did not meet on this occasion.

As to the facilities, in general terms they were excellent as would be expected of a brand-new showpiece London teaching hospital. However, there was no operating theatre with X-ray imaging equipment installed for endovascular interventions. The endovascular operations that had been undertaken at UCLH to this point had been carried out in the radiology department. These included endovascular repair of aortic aneurysms. The lack of adequate facilities for endovascular surgery was the first and most important major deficiency that would have to be corrected in term of facilities if the hospital authorities were serious about their ambitions for an enhanced vascular service. But, it was clear also that there needed to be new appointments in addition to my own in order to build an effective team.

At this point I was not certain whether the intentions of those the top of the UCLH executive ladder were sufficiently serious to invest the sort of money that would be required. More importantly, having just liberated myself from the stranglehold of the NHS and its overbearing bureaucracy, did I really want to sacrifice my newly won freedom so soon, if ever again? I had named my boat, 'Free Spirit' for a reason and new exciting adventures on the high seas were beckoning. With this background of uncertainty I set about preparing a proposal for submission to Andy Webb. I did not hold back. I did not need the job and I was not sure I wanted it. So, if they wanted me, it would have to be on my terms.

I proposed a vascular service for UCLH focussed upon minimally-invasive image-guided interventions as the treatment of choice generally and a programme for endovascular treatment of complex aortic aneurysms to rival the best in the world. For this we would need a completely new dedicated 'hybrid' operating theatre equipped for both image-guided endovascular and major open surgery. We would also need a greatly enhanced budget for consumables. The average cost of a single bespoke aortic endograft for endovascular repair of a complex aneurysm was in the region of £20,000. Added to that, the many specialised wires, catheters and stents for a single case could be easily in excess of £5000. And then there was the issue of personnel. Without an effective multidisciplinary team of surgeons and radiologists no amount of investment in hardware would be of any value. Significant impact would have to be achieved within a relatively short timescale, meaning there would be no time to train people up. Individuals with established skills and experience would have to be identified and head-hunted. I estimated an initial capital investment of £1.5 – 2M and recurring budget of £10M per year over and above the current expenditure; including a substantial salary for myself. To my great surprise Andy Webb accepted the proposals without any discussion of detail or challenge to the numbers. Presumably he did so with the knowledge and approval of the CEO. When I met with him to finalise the deal, he suggested that it would helpful to promote me, as an outsider, and the project I would lead if the University was to award me a personal chair. He said, he would 'fix it'. I suggested the title Professor of Endovascular Surgery, to distinguish my role from that of the existing UCL Professor of Vascular Surgery, George Hamilton, who was based at The Royal Free Hospital.

UCLH and The Royal Free are within the same NHS administrative area of North Central London and both are integral parts of University College London Medical Faculty. Blissfully unaware at this point of long-standing antipathy between the vascular units of these institutions, it occurred to me that it would be good to establish a working relationship with the Royal Free Hospital from the outset. Accordingly, I contacted the Professor Hamilton, to propose a meeting.

I knew George reasonably well. He had succeeded me as President of the Vascular Society and he had visited us in Liverpool with a radiology colleague after referring a patient for treatment of a complex aneurysm. I had found him to be good company and thought of him as one of the 'good guys'. He agreed to meet and proposed a rendezvous in a bar on the South Bank. I thought this a bit strange. Why not meet in his office or at the university? In the event, it very soon became apparent that he had had no desire to meet at all. To summarise his position; cooperation was out of the question and the best thing I could do was to get back on the train to Liverpool! It was not the reaction I had expected. As the local politics became clearer to me, I was able to put his hostility into some context, but it would be an understatement to say that I was both surprised and dismayed by this initial reaction. Sadly, relations between us did not improve with time either. A couple of years later, when we both happened to be invited speakers at a conference in Houston, Texas, I ran into him in a bar. It seemed like a good bridge-building opportunity so I made an effort to engage with him in a spirit of peace and reconciliation. He responded by likening me to a 'paid whore' and I realised I was wasting my time. His antipathy towards me ran very deep.

The fact that my arrival on the scene was not welcomed by the powerful establishment, which George Hamilton represented, was not a good omen. It might seem strange but, for reasons I don't fully understand myself, far from being deterred by this I was even more determined to press ahead.

So, what was this antagonism all about? Well, there was definitely some resentment towards me, as someone arriving from the stix, thinking I could out-do the vascular elite of London. I definitely did not think of my project in those terms at all but was accused of arrogance. Had it just been a matter of discord between individuals the probability is that I could have dealt with it and George Hamilton's antipathy would have been irrelevant. But, I soon discovered there was more to it than that. What George knew full well, and I did not, was that a new round of NHS rationalisation was imminent, encompassing vascular services, with the certain outcome there would be just one hospital in North Central London providing these services to the whole of the sector in the future. He knew this because he was a member of the committee set up by NHS London to prepare the recommendations. As far as Hamilton was concerned, there was only one contender and that was The Royal Free. And then, UCLH decided to compete and head-hunted me for the job. It would have been nice, to have been forewarned what I was being lured into but I was totally naive and not sufficiently savvy to realise that for UCLH to be so willing to invest such a large amount of money there had to be a stronger motive than was at first apparent. To the Royal Free and George Hamilton, in particular, this amounted to a declaration of war and I was on the front line. When it did become clear that my main mission, and in all probability the only one that really mattered to the Trust executives, was to make the case for UCLH to be the regional vascular surgery centre for North Central London, I was not unduly perturbed. Had I known before I would not have taken it on, but I was now committed and decided to follow it through to the best of my ability. What followed was a high-stakes conflict that cruelly exposed my lack of guile.

All of that was to come. Meantime, we had bought a quaint 16th century house in the small village of Flaunden in the Chiltern Hills, with easy railway access to both Euston and Marylebone stations. The house cost us an 'arm and a leg' just before the financial crash which promptly saw property prices tumble. The house in Liverpool remained unsold, but I had a generous salary and we managed financially.

I began work at UCLH on 1st April 2008. At the start I was clear in my own mind that my principal role was to provide the necessary administrative lead to ensure effective implementation of the proposals laid out in the document submitted to Andy Webb. Consistent with my intention not to become embroiled once more in front-line clinical practice, my contract excluded any out of hours on-call commitment. However, it was important to provide clinical leadership and this demanded that I engaged actively in the day-to-day work of the unit. As it turned out, holding together an effective clinical team proved to be my greatest challenge and my greatest failure.

When I arrived, Obi and Chris were functioning pretty much independently of each other. There were no joint ward rounds and communication was mainly on a need-to-know basis. In other words they were not functioning as a team. Once I had a feel for how things were being done, I decided to undertake daily ward rounds of all the patients myself. It was a way of keeping a track of, and coordinating, what was going on. I envisaged an integrated service with an ethos of shared ownership and debate between the consultants about individual patient management that had worked so well in Liverpool. I started my rounds at 7.30 each morning with the junior staff and students. Chris was content with this arrangement because his commitments elsewhere did not allow him to see his NHS patients every day. Obi, on the other hand, was not at all happy and soon made his feelings clear. He strongly resented my 'interference' with his patients, who he considered to be his sole responsibility. I attempted to diffuse his objections by suggesting we did joint ward rounds together, and they did actually happen for a time until he found more important things to do. Consequently, my attempt at team-building backfired seriously.

It had been a bad start and my relations with Obi took a further turn for the worse, subsequently, when I called him at home one evening about a problem with a patient. I cannot recall the details but it must have been something fairly serious for me to call him out of normal working hours. Whatever it was, he was furious and, the next day, made a formal complaint about me to the medical director, Andy Webb. As a result, the two of us were summoned to appear before a panel of five of the most senior consultants in the hospital, a week later. It did not take the panel long to work out that Obi's complaint was symptomatic of underlying deep-rooted opposition to my way of doing things. The end result was that Obi was told to make up his mind whether he was going to support me and the project I had been appointed to lead, or not. The implication being that if the answer was no he should consider applying for another job. Although the panel had backed me, the incident served only to intensify Obi's antipathy towards me. It was a difficult situation and one that I never managed to resolve.

Another incident that occurred in the first year, which remains imprinted in my memory, concerned one of Chris Bishop's celebrity patients; an internationally renowned writer and playwright. He had an unusual aneurysm, that none of us had seen before. It was situated on the main artery supplying blood to the intestines. Minimally invasive endovascular treatment was not possible and open abdominal surgery was the only option. But, it was a tricky proposition; one of those one-off situations of which none of us had previous experience and that posed conspicuous technical challenges and risks. To my great consternation, Chris asked if I would like to take it on. It was an invitation I could hardly refuse. I had been in post for no more than a few weeks and my credibility was on the line. On the day of the surgery, the whole team gathered in the operating theatre to witness the event and to see, if I would 'pass the test'. Fortunately, both the patient and I survived unscathed. Later, the patient wrote in his famous diaries, "The technical description of the aneurysm is a dissection of the superior mesenteric artery. Since its location is unique, before the operation, I ask the surgeon if I can give my name to this particular spot. He is not encouraging, perhaps having thoughts of that for himself. It's a pity. '(His name) Dissection' sounds rather good, I think as I drift off (under anaesthetic)."

What with the issues I had with Obi, Chris's reluctance to engage with the endovascular programme and the fact that the senior interventional radiologist had taken himself off for two year's sabbatical in Barbados, it was plainly apparent that building a credible endovascular team, capable of managing complex aneurysms in the timescale I had set myself, was going to be an even bigger challenge than I had imagined. We needed a high-flyer on the radiology side in the 'Richard McWilliams' mould. And I desperately needed additional surgical help. Someone who would 'buy into' my vision and upon whom I could rely for support. I had no idea where these individuals were going to come from and then I had a stroke of luck, or so it seemed.

I heard on the grapevine that Krassi Ivancev, a very well-known and highly respected, interventional radiologist had fallen out with the regime at his hospital in Malmo, Sweden, and that he was looking to move. Krassi was one of a small group of people that included Tim Chuter and Roy Greenberg in the United States and Michael Lawrence-Brown and David Hartley in Australia, whose pioneering work on endovascular repair of aortic aneurysms had been funded by the Cook Company in the United States from the earliest days. The Cook 'Zenith' Endograft was the market leader in devices for treatment of complex aortic aneurysms. Bulgarian by birth, Krassi had escaped from his native country, as a young doctor, when it was a part of the communist block and he had ended up in Sweden. There, he requalified in medicine and went on to specialise in radiology. Highly driven, energetic and ambitious, he soon made an impression within the rapidly developing speciality of interventional radiology. He was an early disciple of 'mad' Charlie Dotter who was experimenting with crude endovascular treatments in the 70s and 80s and worked with him for a while in Seattle. Back in Sweden, Krassi built up an interventional radiology unit of international renown. Uncompromising and with great self-belief, he continued to innovate, pushing constantly at the technical limits of the speciality. We had invited him to Liverpool to assist us with our first endovascular treatment of an aneurysm of the aorta in the chest and, following this initial contact, one of our trainees, Rao Vallabhaneni, went to work with him in Malmo before taking up a consultant appointment in Liverpool. Richard McWilliams and I also visited Malmo to carry out some animal work in Krassi's research laboratories. Therefore, when I heard the rumour that he was no longer happy in Malmo, I gave him a call. Straight away, he was interested. We arranged to meet up in London. I showed him around the hospital and introduced him to Andy Webb. Andy liked him and quickly sorted out the details necessary to secure his appointment. Krassi joined us to lead the interventional radiology component of the project, within just a few weeks. It was a major breakthrough.

There was no obvious candidate to be headhunted for the consultant surgical post. I needed an academic surgeon. Someone to coordinate research and write papers in addition to doing the surgery. Academic success would be just as important as clinical success to our project and, considering the long timescale of most research projects, we needed to hit the ground running. Miracle cures, while wonderful for the patients concerned, are of little value in respect of the reputation of any surgical service unless the outside world is aware of them. The Daily Mail Medical Section is one avenue for publicising such achievements but well-received publications in respected peer-reviewed scientific journals would count most with the people we needed to impress.

Accordingly, having secured University approval, I advertised for a surgical senior lecturer. There were few applicants and only two, worthy of serious consideration. One, Toby Richards, I knew having met him during the course of a vascular surgery congress in Colorado. We had skied a few pistes together. On paper, he looked good. He had been to Australia to gain experience in endovascular aneurysm repair at a leading centre in Melbourne and had an excellent academic track record for someone at his stage of his career. Accordingly, he got the job.

We had been allocated space in the day-case surgery unit for construction of a new vascular hybrid operating theatre and Krassi and I set about working with architects on a design. Krassi's input to the project at this stage was invaluable.

He had many innovative and ingenious design ideas. It was a superb space on the second floor of the building with big windows overlooking Euston Road and Gower Street.

We had ambitious aims to create an ideal environment for our work encompassing both minimally invasive image-guided interventions and major open surgery. What made it different from a standard operating theatre was the incorporation of high-definition digital X-ray imaging equipment. Krassi and I travelled together to leading manufacturers in Germany and France, to find the best equipment that could be afforded within the budget we had been set. Planning and provisioning involved not only architects but also hospital engineers, infection control experts, senior nursing staff and, of course, finance officers. By the time, we finally secured executive approval for construction to begin, more than a year had gone by and it took the best part of another year for completion of the building work. On December 12th 2009, the 'Evening Standard' reported that the celebrated writer and playwright, Mr Alan Bennett, had opened, at University College Hospital, a brand-new state-of-the-art hybrid operating theatre that would facilitate innovative treatment of dangerous and debilitating vascular diseases without major surgery.

With the team in place, and the hybrid operating theatre fully operational, the programme really started to roll. Krassi's unrestrained enthusiasm and his worldwide reputation were important assets from the start. Within a short time, patients were being referred to UCLH from all parts of the Country. The challenges presented by many of the patients invited technical experimentation in which Krassi revelled and there were, seemingly, no challenges he could not rise to. Within a short time, we had amassed the largest series of complex aortic endografting procedures in the UK.

Chapter 12
Maelstrom

The first signs of serious trouble ahead occurred early on as we were setting up
the complex aortic aneurysm programme. Quite how serious the trouble would
prove to be in the long run was not at all apparent at the time and the incident
soon passed.

Our patients were almost entirely tertiary referrals, which is to say, they were
referred to us by other established vascular consultants who either considered the
risks of intervention, in their own hands, to be too high or had decided that the
complexity of the intervention required, exceeded their technical abilities. In
order to make the greatest impact in the shortest possible time, it was agreed
policy to target this group of patients specifically. However, it was inherently
very high-risk surgery and we were walking a fine line between benefiting
patients and doing them harm. To ensure that we did not cross this line I proposed
for discussion a protocol for detailed risk assessment of patients and precisely
defined selection criteria for surgery. The aim was simple and uncontroversial;
to be certain that the risk of death and disability associated with the treatment did
not exceed those associated with the natural history of the disease itself. I was
totally confounded, therefore, by Krassi's response, which was not only
uncompromisingly negative but openly hostile. He would not be constrained by
any such protocol but would continue to make his own decisions as he always
had done. He clearly considered that his judgement, based as it was on vast
experience, was being impugned and he was deeply affronted. I explained that
nobody was trying to infringe his freedom of practice and that I was simply
asking for his input into the process. He was just not interested. Either, he was
averse to protocols or his reaction was down to 'personality'. I decided to let it
go. I felt sure that he would follow a similar pathway to that defined by the
protocol, in any case, and I didn't, for a second, imagine there would be any

detriment to patients associated with his refusal to cooperate. The incident was, however, disturbing on a personal level. I appended the unmodified risk-assessment protocol and the selection criteria for surgery to our standing operating procedures for everyone else's guidance and forgot about it.

As Director of the service, my responsibilities included audit and quality control. For the reasons I have described, a high mortality rate was to be expected in our cohort of complex aneurysm patients but after two years of the project, and with sufficient numbers to draw reliable conclusions, it had climbed to an alarming 25 per cent. One in four of the patients were dying without ever leaving the hospital. Additionally the incidence of severe life-changing complications, including paraplegia, kidney failure and amputation was also extremely high. It was a new team and the learning curve had been steep but it was apparent also that Krassi's decision-making had diverged considerably from the published protocol. Rarely did he turn down patients for surgery and it seemed there were few challenges he could resist taking on irrespective of the risks. Because of his renown Krassi was definitely a considerable asset to the complex aortic aneurysm programme but, at this point, I worried that he could also be a liability. He was *de facto* running the programme on a day-to-day basis and was primarily responsible for the outcomes achieved. Although he seemed completely unfazed when I showed him the data I reasoned that he would probably make some changes in response. While I was pondering this, two incidents occurred that increased the imperative for action. First, a newspaper article appeared in the Daily Telegraph high-lighting the fact that in some UK hospitals, the mortality rate from treatment of aortic aneurysms was as high as seven per cent and that with an average of five per cent, the results across the country as a whole compared extremely badly with those of continental Europe, where the average was only two per cent. It was certainly true that we were dealing with a much higher risk population of patients but, if the UCLH data were to enter into the public domain, we would be condemned, quite rightly, for a mortality rate so far in excess of the norm. And, there was no guarantee of improvement with a wait and see policy. The risk to the reputation of the hospital was a relatively minor consideration compared to the welfare of the patients themselves but it was an added pressure to act sooner rather than later.

The second incident was truly cataclysmic and a critical turning point. Krassi had taken an instant dislike to Toby from the start when he arrived on the scene and would not abide him in his operating theatre. This was a serious problem for

Toby because he had been appointed specifically to work on the complex aneurysm programme. Krassi had issues with Obi also but tolerated him in preference to Toby. Consequently, relations between Obi and Toby were not good either.

The animosity that had been building progressively between Krassi and Toby eventually spilt over into bitter conflict. Ironically, when the hostilities really kicked off I had organised a special event designed to promote peace and harmony within the team. It was to be a weekend of sailing and socialising in the South of France, where I had a holiday home. Additional accommodation had been arranged for those that could not be put up at the house and I chartered a yacht, in addition to my own, so that everyone would have the chance to sail. The whole team was invited. Toby was on-call and could not come. Obi, for his own reasons, declined the invitation. Carole and I had gone ahead a few days earlier to make preparations. Everyone else was due to arrive at Toulon airport on Saturday morning where I would pick them up.

On Friday morning, I received an urgent telephone call from Toby. A patient Krassi had operated upon on Monday had got into trouble and was doing badly. Investigation, two days after the operation, had revealed the problem to be acute mesenteric ischaemia. The blood supply to the bowel had been cut off during the course of the procedure. As the surgeon on-call, Toby had taken the patient back to theatre to see what could be done but he found it was too late to do anything. The bowel was no longer viable. Assuming that the blood supply to the gut had been cut off two days ago this was not surprising. Toby closed the patient up again, knowing that his condition would continue to deteriorate and that he would die. Krassi, doubting Toby's competence and judgement demanded a second surgical opinion. Chris then became involved. On Thursday, Toby and Chris took the patient back to theatre again together for another look. The intestines by this time were totally black. The two surgeons agreed that there was nothing anyone could do and that the patient's condition was terminal. Krassi was still unwilling to accept that this was the case and demanded yet another surgical exploration which Toby refused to organise. A bitter and violent row ensued which prompted Toby to call me in France.

The position seemed clear to me. Bowel ischaemia is a rapidly fatal condition and the patient's fate was almost certainly sealed by the time the diagnosis was made 48 hours or more, after the primary intervention. Moreover, Toby's findings had been confirmed by Chris, an extremely experienced and highly competent vascular surgeon. Krassi would just have to accept that the patient's condition was terminal. When I called him, he went ballistic. How could I possibly side with anyone as inexperienced and clueless as Toby? He informed me that, as far as he was concerned, not only was the trip to France off but he was considering resigning. I let him cool off for an hour or two, then called him back. Very reluctantly, he agreed to come to France. It turned out later that he had arranged with Chris Bishop to fly directly from France to North Africa to examine one of Chris's private patients who happened to be the king of Saudi Arabia. Had this not been the case, I doubt if he would have changed his mind. He and Chris had made their own travel arrangements and arrived some time before the others. Carole and I sat down with Krassi and his wife, Eva, and I opened a bottle of nicely chilled rosé wine in the hopes that it might cool his anger. But, it was hopeless, he remained fixated on what he perceived to be my backing for Toby against him. I tried to explain that my decision had nothing to do with backing anyone but was based on the facts of the case as I understood them. He would not accept this, and progress towards any more meaningful conversation was impossible.

It was now abundantly clear that the situation was totally out of control. We were on a rapidly downward spiral. I was sitting on incendiary outcome data and my team members were engaged in all-out war with each other. The UCLH vascular project was on the verge of implosion. All of the key issues centred around Krassi, but I simply could not get through to him. I needed help and I decided to call the Medical Director. Had Andy Webb still been around, there might have been a chance of sorting something out. However, he had been headhunted for a job in Canada a few months previously and his place had been taken by an anaesthetist called Geoff Bellingham. Geoff was a considerably less decisive character and still new to the job.

So, it was on the Saturday morning, while waiting at the airport for the rest of the weekend party to arrive, that I called Geoff Bellingham. After I had described the situation, he asked me what I thought should be done. I told him we should pause the complex aneurysm programme temporarily to review the policies and procedures, specifically in respect of patient selection criteria, and to try to sort out the interpersonal relationship issues. I suggested that this could be done quietly, without drawing too much attention to ourselves. He grasped the seriousness of the situation straight away and agreed that we would meet to discuss details, early in the following week. He did say, however, that he would have to inform the CEO, Sir Robert Naylor in the meantime. This I did not want. Support, financial and otherwise, has a habit of drying up when the upper echelons of hospital management perceive that a service has become dysfunctional. However, Geoff Bellingham was adamant.

For the remainder of the weekend Krassi avoided further contact with me while engaging in intense hushed conversations with everyone else. Despite his ill-concealed hostility towards me and my own mounting anxiety at the unfolding events, everyone else seemed to have a good time and the weekend passed surprisingly well.

Back in London, Toby knew what was going on but Obi was totally in the dark. When he heard the programme had been suspended, he was furious. I could understand his anger because, in all the turmoil, I had not communicated the decision to him directly as I should have done. Back in London, I tried to apologise and to explain my reasons but his already deep antipathy towards me became absolute and placed him firmly in the Krassi camp against me. As far as Krassi was concerned, he took the whole thing very personally. His competence had been impugned twice in as many days. The Rubicon had been well, and truly, crossed and what had previously been low-level non-cooperation, morphed abruptly into bitter enmity.

Things had started out well enough between Krassi and me. We dined at each other's houses and he entertained us with the chilling story of his escape from communist Bulgaria, crossing the border under the noses of the border guards in the dead of night. That, he had achieved so much success subsequently, against difficult odds evinced a highly driven character, which should perhaps have alerted me to potential personality issues more than it did, at the time. I discovered, subsequently, that he had left Malmo under a cloud having being replaced, against his will, as director of the vascular service. There had been some dispute or other but I never knew the details. Initially, he was supportive and offered me lots of good advice on development of the service generally and the design of the new hybrid theatre in particular. For a while we had a good working partnership and undertook the first complex aortic procedures together. He was considerably more experienced and skilled than I, at manipulating wires and catheters around the body guided by X-ray images on a screen. This was his stock-in-trade whereas mine was surgery with a scalpel. However, his style of operating was very different to mine. He was excitable and dictatorial. The operations were often long and difficult, some taking more than 12 hours, and when the going got tough, the atmosphere would become tense and sometimes fraught. Despite this, there was no denying Krassi's persistence. From the perspective of the patients the problem was that, although the interventions themselves were minimally-invasive, the strain on their physiology of prolonged general anaesthesia was considerable. And, most were elderly and frail. The risk of inadvertent damage to critical blood vessels associated with technically very demanding procedures was relatively high also. There never was any question of impugning Krassi's technical skill at any time. He was exceptionally gifted. But, after a time it was clear that our temperaments in the theatre were incompatible and we stopped operating together.

I was convinced that I had made the right decision to suspend the complex aneurysm programme but the problem I had now, was how to prevent the whole UCLH vascular project from disintegrating. With two main players, and especially Krassi, set against me; my leadership credentials were seriously under question. Nevertheless, I had a job to do and had to press on. I needed help and it was clear Geoff Bellingham was not capable of providing it. Mediation by someone with the capability to undertake an independent review of the programme and to make recommendations for reform seemed to be the best option. I consulted with the President and Chairman of the audit committee of the Vascular Society who agreed that this would be the best way forward. However, they regarded the affair to be an internal matter for UCLH and did not want the Society to be involved. Whoever was chosen for the job would have to command the respect of all concerned, Krassi included and Tim Chuter's name came to mind. He seemed to fit the bill exactly. Accordingly he was the person I recommended to Geoff Bellingham to conduct the review. Geoff acquiesced and asked me to prepare a summary of the position, including up-to-date mortality and morbidity data, to be appended to a formal request which he would dispatch. Tim willingly agreed to accept the assignment and flew from San Francisco to London to begin work within days.

On paper, there was no one better qualified than Tim to do this review. He had more knowledge and experience of the esoteric world of complex endovascular aneurysm repair than anyone on the planet. He was, and is, totally straight, honest and objective. He is also a very nice guy and this was a problem! Being friends with both Krassi and myself, he carefully avoided to drawing conclusions that were invidious to either of us. Consequently, his report was anodyne and criticised no one. He acknowledged that our complication rate, and especially the mortality rate, was high, but this, he said was because we were operating upon an exceptionally high-risk group of patients; a conclusion that was indisputably self-evident. He found no evidence to suggest that the operative procedures were not being undertaken with appropriate skill or expertise but this was not a point of contention either. Tim avoided, completely, any judgement about the protocols we had put in place for risk assessment; whether the selection criteria for surgery were appropriate and whether or not, they were being followed. Having failed to address these critical issues, he was not in a position to make any substantive recommendations on these points either. It was extremely frustrating from my perspective. Krassi, on the other hand, felt he had been vindicated. The terms of reference for the review prepared by Geoff Bellingham, which he had not shared with me beforehand, were vague in the extreme, possibly intentionally so, and he was happy to accept the report as it stood. As far as he was concerned it served the purpose of pouring oil on troubled water. Tim had not condemned the programme outright. That was good enough for him and it was clear that he had no intention of taking the matter, any further.

Nothing had been resolved in respect of operational protocols. Nor had the issue of fraught interpersonal relationships been addressed. If the complex aneurysm programme was to be salvaged we had to get it restarted as soon as possible but there was still no agreement as how this should be done and on what terms. Indeed, there was some uncertainty as to whether there was still a collective will for it to continue and my first task was to ascertain that there was indeed a positive consensus on this fundamental question. I then had to set about trying, once more, to find a formula that might work. I produced a new set of draft proposals for discussion at a series of difficult meetings. They included revised guidelines on patient selection with additional objective physiological and anatomical tests for risk assessment and new operating team arrangements.

As things stood there was no prospect of Krassi and I undertaking cases together and he would not work with Toby. Therefore, the only option was to separate into two teams, with access to the operating theatre on different days of the week. It was a very unsatisfactory compromise, but the best that could be achieved, and one that was accepted. To pacify Krassi, I proposed that he be formerly recognised as clinical lead for the complex aneurysm programme on the understanding that he would conform to the new risk-assessment guidelines we had agreed upon. I would be primarily responsible for everything else. None of this pleased me personally and I was particularly unhappy to be effectively excluded from the programme I had set up as the flagship of the new UCLH vascular service. However, it was the price that had to be paid for peace, or a temporary truce at least. After eight weeks of suspension, I recommended to Geoff Bellingham that the programme be recommenced, working to the newly agreed protocols and operating arrangements.

I had no great expectations that everything would go swimmingly, thereafter. Krassi, was never going to accept the concept of collective responsibility, nor be constrained by operational protocols. The mortality figures did improve but the programme itself was now mortally wounded. I had bought a little more time, but that was all. Toby accepted that he was going to be denied access to complex endovascular work and forged new pathways for himself in carotid artery surgery.

Personal day-to-day communication between myself and Krassi and Obi virtually ceased. The rare occasions when Krassi and I did meet to talk, were strained at best. One such was in New York. We were both on the programme of the Annual Veith meeting in November 2011. During the week before, I had had a conversation with Chris Bishop, the one person upon whom I could count for support throughout. We were discussing Obi who was, by this time, openly hostile and behaving in an aggressively obstructive manner towards me. Basically, I wanted Chris to have a word with Obi on my behalf. In Chris's view the situation was hopeless and he suggested I should consider building a case against Obi to get rid of him for good. My position as Clinical Lead for vascular surgery gave me no power to hire or fire anyone. I could make a recommendation to the Trust Authorities who do have that power but the recommendation would have to be formally justified. To get rid of Obi would require evidence of wrongdoing or serious and irremediable clinical incompetence. I quickly dismissed the idea. He was diligent in respect of his clinical practice and my own position was so weakened, by then, that an attempt to have him sanctioned on grounds of non-cooperation or insubordination would be likely to back fire against me. Somehow, Obi and, therefore, Krassi got wind of this conversation and Krassi confronted me about it in New York. We met in the bar of The Hilton Hotel in Times Square, where the conference was being held. The conversation went something like this:

Krassi: I hear you are planning to sack Obi.

Me: You are misinformed, there isn't and never has been, any plan to sack Obi.

Krassi: If you do sack Obi, I will quit.

Me: There are no plans to sack Obi.

Krassi: I am thinking of quitting anyway.

Me: We are in a bad place. I am willing to discuss any proposals you might have to make things better but if you think you can put a gun to my head to get your way, forget it, because I will not respond to threats.

Probably, I could and should have handled this conversation better but it was an emotionally charged encounter on both sides and neither of us behaved with great credit.

The incident did nothing to improve matters, either for the programme or for me, personally. The sharks were circling, closing in for the kill.

I guess within a short time after this incident, or possibly even before, Krassi had made his first overtures to George Hamilton at The Royal Free or maybe, it was the other way around. I have no way of knowing. What is certain, is that they had forged a secret deal. This first became apparent when patients listed for treatment at UCLH started disappearing off the UCLH waiting list. Krassi, without telling anyone – not the waiting list clerk, not the vascular surgery manager, not the Medical Director and certainly not me – was taking patients off the UCLH list to operate upon them at The Royal Free. For this to happen, he had to have been given operating rights and this could not have happened without the collusion of the senior executives at The Royal Free. When I went to the Medical Director with this, I had expected outrage and an immediate dramatic response but he seemed barely interested. Apparently, he could not care less. I could not believe it! Either, he was too weak to do anything or, as seems more likely in retrospect, he already knew something that I didn't. Something I would find out to my cost in due course.

Chapter 13
Jack Vause

He had not been able to pee properly and that had been the start of it. He needed to 'go' too often and when the urge came, he had had to be quick about it. There was a constant 'dribble' patch in his underpants. His doctor diagnosed an enlarged prostate gland and referred him to his local hospital in Chertsey for keyhole surgery. The aortic aneurysm was an incidental finding on an ultrasound scan undertaken to examine his kidneys.

Jack Vause was 78, and had been retired from his labouring job with the local council, for nearly 20 years. He lived in a small terraced house in Addlestone with his wife Doreen who was about the same age. She had suffered with her health for years as a consequence of crippling arthritis and depended heavily on Jack for nearly everything. She had a stairlift and a wheelchair for outdoors but getting from room to room or visiting the toilet involved major effort. Jack's own health had been reasonable but he was not as strong as he used to be and his struggles to cope with Doreen's needs were not helped by the aches and pains, which he put down to old age. Other than the problems with his bladder, he did not have any specific symptoms and was not only bewildered but also alarmed when he was told he needed to see a vascular surgeon urgently.

The local vascular surgeon was Neil Browning. Originating from South Africa, he had been to the United States for training in open surgery for thoracoabdominal aortic aneurysms before coming to the UK. As one of a small number of surgeons in the UK with experience of these big operations, he was all too familiar with the challenges and risks involved and was keen to explore the potential benefits of the newly developing minimally-invasive endovascular alternatives. Accordingly he approach us at UCLH with a view to working with us. This suited us because he was the source of many patients and provided valuable additional expertise.

Neil turned up at a one of our Friday lunchtime vascular unit meetings with scans of Jack's aneurysm. It was big. From the upper chest, it extended all the way down to the end of the aorta in the lower abdomen, with involvement of the branches to all of the internal abdominal organs.

Technically, it was 'treatable' with a Tim Chuter type of branched endograft and it was decided that Jack should undergo detailed risk assessment. The test results revealed issues with his heart, his lungs and his kidney function which would have certainly excluded conventional open surgery, if this had been his only option. The term 'minimally-invasive' belied the fact that, although endovascular repair of Jack's extensive complex aneurysm would involve less surgical trauma than an open operation, it would nevertheless, be a major undertaking in an elderly man with pre-existing frailties. None of his results actually crossed any of the red lines of our selection protocol but the overall risk of perioperative death, was in the range from five to ten per cent, and therefore borderline. Set against this the risk of him dying from rupture of his aneurysm within the next 12 months was in the order of 25 per cent. On the face of it the balance of risks was in favour of surgery but it was an unenviable choice. The final say would be up to Jack and Doreen and Neil arranged to see them in his clinic at Chertsey to talk through the risks and benefits with them. No doubt they struggled to know what to do for the best, with added fear as to what would happen to Doreen if he should die. They chose, what appeared to be the least risky option; they chose surgery, no doubt with considerable trepidation.

It needed a complicated endograft composed of three separate sections to be connected together to form a continuous tube within the aneurysm. The middle section had branches for connection to the natural branches to the kidneys, liver, spleen and intestines in the abdomen. It had to be made to measure to match Jack's anatomy precisely.

Paraplegia is a devastating complication of all forms of surgical repair of extensive aneurysms like Jack's. Most patients in whom it occurs do not survive but those who do, are left with paralysed legs and urinary and faecal incontinence for the rest of their lives. The risk is present because the spinal cord is supplied by an artery, the artery of Adamkiewicz, which arises from an intercostal branch of the aorta just above the diaphragm. In the conventional open operation the intercostal artery bearing the artery of Adamkiewicz can be incorporated into the graft. But, it is too small to be connected into an endograft and those like Jack face a higher risk of paraplegia as a price to be paid for a minimally-invasive operation. In fact there is sufficient blood supply to the spinal cord from other arteries to compensate for loss of the artery of Adamkiewicz in most patients but, for the few in whom there is not, disaster lies in store.

Occasionally, the blood supply to the spinal cord is reduced only temporarily during or immediately after the operation when the blood pressure is low. In these patients, paraplegia can be prevented or even reversed by drawing off the clear fluid that normally surrounds the spinal cord within its canal in the spine. This is effective because blood flowing into the spinal cord is dependant not only on the pressure pushing it forward but also on the pressure of the spinal fluid, which resists forward flow. Changing the balance of pressures by boosting that of the blood and reducing that of the spinal fluid increases the blood flow to the spinal cord. It was our routine, therefore, for all patients to have a cannula inserted into the spinal canal to enable the spinal fluid to be drawn off during and after surgery. Despite this, a few patients did still develop paraplegia. Krassi, who had an undeniable talent for invention, came up with an ingenious plan designed to further reduce the risk. He instructed the manufacturer of the endograft to construct an additional short branch in the middle section of the endograft. The idea was to allow pressurised blood to pass into the aneurysm sac and to perfuse the small spinal artery during the critical post-operative period while the blood pressure was low. The branch was closed off with a plug at a second, minor operation under local anaesthetic when the patient's condition was stable, a few days later. This last step finally excluded the aneurysm from the circulation completely. Jack's endograft included this additional detail.

The most complex operations took place in the hybrid operating theatre midweek, on Wednesdays; one patient usually taking up the whole of the day. Although Jack was delivered to the theatre, just before 8.30, it was 10 o'clock before he was anaesthetised and all preparations were in place for the operation to begin. After completing my daily 7.30 am ward round, I met with Krassi and Obi and junior members of the operating team to review the images of Jack's aneurysm on a computer screen and to go over the plan of attack. The three sections of the endograft were to be introduced into the aneurysm through plastic sheaths, a little under a centimetre in diameter. These sheaths would be inserted into the femoral arteries in the groins. The upper segment would go in first, followed by the middle section bearing the branches. The middle section would be overlapped inside the upper section to make a seal. With these two pieces in place, another sheath would be inserted into the artery to the left arm just beneath the collarbone and through this sheath stents would be introduced and guided into place to connect the branches of the endograft to the four natural arteries supplying the liver and spleen, the two kidneys and the intestines. Once all the branches had been connected; the third, lower, section of the endograft would be deployed. This last piece was trouser-shaped with two branches to fit into the main arteries to the legs. All of these manoeuvres would be completed remotely, guided by X-ray images on big screens mounted above the operating table. The branched section of the endograft had small radio-opaque metal markers incorporated to mark to the position of the openings into the branches on the screens. It was going to be a painstaking process. An exercise in manual dexterity guided by real-time images displayed on a screen like a complex computer game. A computer game in which a life lost would be real.

Exactly how long the procedure would take, could not be accurately predicted. It depended how difficult or easy it was to manipulate the guidewires and catheters into the branches of the endograft and then, into the natural branches in order to deliver the connecting stents. It can take anything from four to twelve hours. During this time, the sheaths in the femoral arteries would block most of the blood flow into the legs. A number of previous patients had suffered acute gangrene as a result and had had to have their legs amputated. To eliminate this risk, the plan was to create a temporary bypass to carry blood from the right arm into the legs around the blocking sheaths. This would be the first step.

So, shortly after 10 am, Jack's anaesthetised naked body was painted with bright orange iodine antiseptic and covered with sterile blue drapes. Windows over both groins and beneath both collarbones were sealed with self-adherent transparent film. The first part of the procedure, the bypass, was conventional surgery. Obi and I shared this work, assisted by a registrar and a senior house officer. The femoral arteries in both groins and the subclavian arteries to both arms were exposed and dissected out. I stitched one end of a long Dacron fabric tube graft to the subclavian artery on the right side. At its lower end, the tube divided into two limbs, to be joined to the femoral arteries. Once this was completed blood flowed through these tubes from the right arm into both legs outside of the body. They would be the main source of blood supply to the legs after the sheaths had been inserted. A short length of Dacron tube graft was joined, also to the left subclavian artery. A sheath would be introduced through this graft and into the aorta from above for passage of the connecting stents to the abdominal branches.

With this first step completed, we changed into radiation protective clothing, leaded aprons and spectacles with leaded glass lenses. Krassi joined the operating team at this point.

The X-ray machine, which had been pushed back previously for the bypass procedure, was now 'dressed' in sterile drapes with an oversized sterile 'shower cap' to cover the 'tube' and it was manoeuvred into place over Jack's body. With a huge arm arching over the operating table, it resembled an enormous robotic praying mantis. Six people clustered around it and the operating table. There were three consultants, Krassi, Obi and myself together with the surgical registrar, the senior house officer and the scrub nurse. At the head of the table the anaesthetist, a German doctor whose name was Bettina, sat in the midst of her machinery with her registrar standing by. The fully motorised X-ray machine was operated by a radiographer standing at a console to one side. Two nurses and the operating department assistant (ODA) were standing by awaiting instructions. The ODA knew where to find the many wires, catheters and other consumables that would be needed over the next few hours. He did an invaluable job because there were hundreds of items stored in sterile packaging in glass-fronted cabinets lining the walls of the room. There were a couple of medical students hovering on the periphery and a representative of the Cook Company that had supplied the endograft. She was there to give technical advice if needed. It was a crowded room and some at the periphery struggled to get a view screens mounted on a gantry above each side of the operating table.

It was after midday, by the time the first guidewire could be seen on the screens, being threaded into Jack's aorta from his groin followed by the sheath through which the endografts would be passed. It did not take long for the first section of the endograft to be deployed in the chest.

Deployment of the second section took a lot longer and did not go well. It needed to be positioned and orientated with its branches lined up exactly with the natural branches of the aorta in order to make the connections. The metal markers on the endograft to guide alignment were confusing and the Cook Company 'rep' proffered advice to ensure that we did not foul-up by misinterpreting them. The markers were not misinterpreted but, as the endograft was advanced into Jack's aneurysm it had rotated through almost 90 degrees. Attempts to correct the resulting misalignment by twisting the sheath were only partially successful and the hard task of connecting the branches with bridging stents had been made many times more difficult.

To manipulate the end of a long floppy guidewire into a small branch, more than a meter away along the tortuous vascular pathway guided by a two-dimensional image on a screen is not easy at the best of times. The wires are passed through long thin catheters with various shapes of bends and hooks at the end to enable the tip of the wire to be directed as it emerges. Once in place, the catheter is advanced into the artery and the soft wire is replaced with a stiffer one, over which the stent can be passed and positioned to complete the connection.

Krassi was normally good at this but he struggled. We did what we could, to assist and to offer opinions or suggestions while he barked out orders to the radiographer, the ODA and everyone else. After four hours of intense concentration only one branch had been connected and the tension in the operating room was high and mounting. The instrument table was covered in a spaghetti-like tangle of discarded wires and catheters. The drapes were soaked with blood leaking around the sheaths in the groins and there was a slowly spreading pool of blood on the floor. I suggested we take a break. When we came back ten minutes or so later, Krassi was calmer. We tided things up stopped the leak around the sheath, covered the stained drapes with clean ones and had the floor mopped. Within an hour of restarting, two more branches were connected and there was just one more to go.

The branch, to the left kidney, was badly positioned due to the rotation of the endograft. It also came off the aorta at an awkward angle and its mouth was narrowed by disease. After another two hours of struggle it was eventually connected but the artery had been damaged by repeated attempts to enter it and the blood supply to most of that kidney was lost. Its function would be seriously impaired but there was nothing that could be done. It took only 30 minutes or so for the third, bifurcated, section of the endograft to be deployed across the division of the aorta into the legs following which final X-rays confirmed that all the connections were intact and that there were no leaks, other than from the extra branch left open to, supply the spinal cord and, hopefully, prevent paraplegia.

We still had the temporary bypass running down the outside of Jacks torso to remove, all the exposed arteries to repair and the wounds to close. It was almost 10 o'clock when all was done. Jack had been on the operating table for 14 hours.

Next morning, he was still unconscious on a ventilator on the intensive care unit. This was planned. However, the next day he was still not showing any sign of waking up despite most of the anaesthetic drugs having been withdrawn. The blood tests showed poor kidney function; not surprising, considering that he had lost most of his left kidney. On the third day, he showed some signs of stirring but had still not opened his eyes and was not responding to commands. He was reacting to painful stimuli, but only on his left side. This was worrying. His right leg was not reacting. The next day Jack was responding to spoken commands but he was still not moving his right arm and leg. A brain scan showed the reason why. He had suffered a stroke. There was damage to the left side of his brain about which nothing could be done. Despite this, he was trying to breathe for himself and ready to come off the ventilator machine. His blood pressure was stable and we decided to take him back to the operating theatre to close off the extra 'spinal' branch of the endograft before allowing him to awake fully. Back on the intensive care unit the remainder of the sedative drugs were stopped and early, the next morning, the breathing tube was withdrawn from his windpipe. Now fully awake, Jack was able to understand what was said to him but could not speak and was still unable to move his right arm and leg.

Twelve weeks later, Jack had regained some speech and movement of his right arm. His leg remained weak but he could stand and take a few steps with a Zimmer frame. He had managed to avoid renal dialysis but his kidney function remained borderline necessitating continued medication and a low protein diet. It was very obvious to everyone, himself included, that he would no longer be able to give to Doreen, the care and support she needed. The one saving grace was that they were eventually accommodated together in a local authority care home where they shared a room.

Jack's story was typical. I don't know how long he lived afterwards but his quality of life was never the same. An important consideration when assessing the benefits of this type of surgery is that most of the patients have no symptoms at all from their aneurysms and are unaware of them until they are 'discovered'. As in Jack's case they are, most often, diagnosed incidentally during the course of an investigation for an unrelated condition. Therefore, there is no question of improving their quality of life, for example by relieving pain or some other disability. This means that the rationale for surgery is predicated entirely on survival. What is the probability that the patient will live longer with an operation compared to without an operation? The relevance of quality of life is that surgery

148

will make it worse. Jack's story exemplified the fact that, although endovascular repair of extensive complex aortic aneurysms may be minimally invasive compared to the open surgical alternative and therefore survivable, it is still a high-risk procedure. For this reason detailed risk assessment is an essential step before a decision is made to offer surgery to a patient.

The risk-assessment protocol, that Krassi had a problem with at UCLH had as its aim an operative mortality rate of 5 percent or less. Ten percent was a threshold that could not justifiably be crossed under any circumstances. When 25 of the first hundred patients treated for complex aortic aneurysms had died and others were left with serious new disabilities it was clear that something had gone seriously wrong. Krassi attributed the bad results to inexperience of the supporting team and intensive care staff and apparently accepted no personal responsibility. It had undoubtedly been a steep learning curve for many in the team but I knew also that the risk-assessment protocol was being totally disregarded. I was waiting to see if the results might improve as the team gained more experience and hoping that Krassi, despite denying liability, would quietly modify his approach in the knowledge of what was, or was not, being achieved. That was before my hand was forced by the events described in the previous chapter.

Chapter 14

An Ignominious Ending

It was not until after I had started work at UCLH that I fully appreciated what a political can of worms I was entering into. It is unlikely there had been any deliberate intent to keep me in the dark but nobody had spelt it out and I had assumed, naively, that the investment in the vascular service was motivated primarily by a desire to bring it up to a standard considered appropriate for an illustrious institution such as UCLH. In reality the executive team knew they were about to be locked into a fierce battle for vascular dominance with their nearest rival, The Royal Free, and that there would be only one winner. George Hamilton was fully up to speed with what was about to happen, which put into context the hostile rejection to my gesture of friendship that had so perplexed me at our meeting in a cafe on the South Bank six months previously.

From the earliest days of institutionalised medicine, there has been intense rivalry between renowned London Teaching Hospitals as they compete with each other for prestige and the wealth from charitable donations that come with it. Long before the inception of the NHS, an established order was in place with a dense concentration of celebrated healing institutions, some within sight of each other. Nearly all are named after some Christian saint, or other, to emphasise their charitable origins as refuges for the sick and destitute. Over the years, as they gained in status and wealth, they established their own idiosyncratic traditions and pride in the illustrious achievements of their most eminent and distinguished physicians and surgeons. Despite the egalitarian credentials of the NHS, few attempts were made to subvert the privileged status and considerable power of these institutions in the early years and they continued to function almost autonomously. However, in the late 1990s, after years of Conservative government austerity had left the NHS in a sorry state with dilapidated Victorian buildings and unacceptably long waiting lists, the Blair government decided to pump money into it. Nearly everyone agreed that this was needed, but serious questions were asked about how the cash was to be spent and what returns the tax-paying public could expect in return. This became a theme adopted by both main political parties and it resulted in the implementation of long-term systematic rationalisation programmes with the laudable aim of better distributing available funds according to the needs of the population. The London teaching hospitals were, finally, in the firing line.

Expensive specialised hospital services, like vascular surgery, were high priority targets for reorganisation. Government claimed that the purpose of rationalisation was not to cut costs but to improve the quality of care. On this occasion they did have a case as far as vascular surgery was concerned. There was a growing body of evidence to show that the best outcomes for patients, especially those with the most complex diseases, were achieved in the highest-volume centres. Therefore, it made sense not only financially but also clinically to concentrate the high-end work, at least, into a smaller number of specialist units. In the provinces, this generally meant one centre in each region and in regions, with just one main teaching hospital, the choice of site was uncontroversial. Where there were two or more teaching institutions with valid claims, there was usually trouble. London, with its cluster of famous teaching hospitals steeped in history and established traditions in vascular surgery, was never going to be easy.

Healthcare services in London are organised on the basis of five wedge-shaped sectors radiating out from the centre. Each sector has an administrative structure equivalent to that of a Region in the provinces. UCLH is at the apex of the North Central Sector on the main University College London campus. The Royal Free is in the middle of the Sector in Hampstead. UCLH did not have a great tradition in vascular surgery in modern times. On the other hand, The Royal Free vascular unit, under the direction of George Hamilton, had become very well established and was highly regarded. It so dominated the scene locally that, two years prior to my appointment, UCLH had offered to cede all vascular services to The Royal Free. The offer was refused by George Hamilton. I suspect that he did not welcome the idea of UCLH consultants working in his institution, such was the antipathy between them. He could be confident that they could never challenge him and it was better therefore to leave them where they were. Against this background it was assumed, by nearly everyone, that the Royal Free Hospital would be the chosen site for the North Central Sector Regional Vascular

Centre. Andy Webb, the Medical Director at UCLH was one who thought otherwise and he persuaded the executive team to invest in a bid to secure the regional centre for his hospital. My appointment followed directly from this decision. When it became apparent to the Royal Free that UCLH was spending significant amounts of money to thwart their aims, they followed suit commissioning a hybrid operating theatre of their own. At a cost two or three times of that spent by UCLH.

Within a year, things started to happen. NHS London set up a Vascular Services Working Group to review existing services and make recommendations for revision. It was chaired jointly by Professor Matt Thompson, Director of vascular services at St George's Hospital in Tooting and Professor Nick Cheshire Director of vascular services at St Mary's Hospital in Paddington. The Working Group had representatives from the other teaching hospitals including George Hamilton from the Royal Free. No one was invited from UCLH. I requested an urgent appointment with the Medical Director of NHS London, Dr Andy Mitchell, who had commissioned the review. Geoff Bellingham, who had just replaced Andy Webb as UCLH Medical Director, accompanied me to a meeting at the NHS London offices, a week later. Andy Mitchell was a welcoming and pleasant man in his early 50s. He listened politely as I pointed out the conflicts of interest intrinsic within the review mechanism he had set up, especially in respect of the chairmen who were hardly likely to be unbiased when it came to making their recommendations, and also the disadvantage accorded to UCLH without any representation at all on the Working Group. While I recognised that it was too late to change the fundamentals, such as replacing the chairmen with someone from outside London, representation of all the main teaching hospitals, UCLH included, would ensure a more fair process. In response, he offered platitudes and reassurances about the objectivity of the exercise and made no concessions, whatsoever. The composition and membership of the Working Group were, he said, matters for the Joint Chairmen to decide. It was clear, I was wasting my time.

When the final report of the London Vascular Services Working Group was published about a year later, I had to admit that it was balanced, evidence-based and rationally argued. I had no issues with it. There was no focus on individual hospitals as I had feared there would be. The main recommendation was that the total number of hospitals in London offering vascular services should be reduced from the 26 that existed at the time to just six. As anticipated, there was to be only one in the North Central Sector but the report indicated that this was a matter to be decided locally. Although no specific hospital was preferred in any sector, given the authorship of the report, it was a fair assumption that St. George's and St Mary's would not miss out in their sectors.

The report was accepted for implementation in full by NHS London and the process of specific site selection was devolved to local Commissioning Authorities. There, then, followed a welcome hiatus before the next step. Welcome to me, at least, because, although the building blocks of the vascular project were all in place towards the end of 2009, we needed more time and more patients to establish UCLH as a credible alternative to The Royal Free.

We were making good progress and the numbers were going up but team cohesion was sadly lacking and a constant worry. Krassi was not happy to work with either Obi or Toby. So he set about creating his own team. We were doing several million pounds worth of business a year with Cook inc., the American Company that manufactured the endovascular devices we were using, and Krassi secured funding from them to support an Endovascular Fellowship; a one-year training post in complex aortic aneurysm repair. The first Fellow appointed was Australian and the second Irish. Both were excellent but they effectively became Krassi's personal assistants to the exclusion of the homegrown UCLH trainees and everyone else. Krassi was establishing for himself a practically autonomous service under his personal control. I had lots of conversations with him at this time to try to find a way forward that we could both be comfortable with. The more we talked, the more it seemed to me that personal ambition was his only driving force and that, to him, UCLH was no more than a means to an end. I detected no sense of loyalty towards the hospital, the project, the team or to me, personally. The challenge for me, therefore, was how to keep him on board so that the project could continue to benefit from his undoubted talents. Meantime, Obi remained antipathetic towards me and Chris, who had little enthusiasm for involvement in the complex aneurysm programme kept away from it completely.

After making good progress initially with the academic programme, this became contentious territory also. Toby, as the senior lecturer, had been appointed with a remit to coordinate research and ensure a regular stream of publications and presentations. Our credibility as a leading vascular centre depended upon it and The Royal Free, with an established academic reputation, had a considerable lead on us at this stage. In terms of innovation, the complex aneurysm programme was by far the most productive area but this was, by now,

Krassi's domain. I failed to persuade him to allow access to Toby, who did not get a look in. Toby, therefore, went off to do his own thing and did good work relating to blood transfusion and carotid artery disease.

Krassi came up with two big ideas for research and development. One related to protection of the spinal cord with the aim of preventing paraplegia. The other was to use carbon dioxide gas in place of conventional X-ray contrast media for intra-operative imaging. Conventional liquid media injected into the circulation, are highly toxic to the kidneys. Kidney failure of varying degrees was a big problem in our patients because of the large volume of contrast media used during the course of long complex operations. Carbon dioxide gas injected into the arteries is radio-opaque and is quickly eliminated by being exhaled from the lungs. It should, in theory at least, be much safer. When we tried it, we found it did not provide images of sufficiently high definition for the most critical parts of the operations and it was still necessary to use quite large volumes of conventional liquid contrast in addition. So, it was not an unqualified success. The key issue was whether or not the use of carbon dioxide gas conferred any benefit at all in terms of post-operative kidney function or was a waste of time and money. So, we decided to undertake a research study to find out.

It was an important study, which we knew would attract a lot of interest. Therefore, we planned to submit an abstract for presentation at the annual meeting of the Vascular Society. A junior trainee was tasked with doing the analysis and she presented the results to the team on the day before an abstract was due to be submitted. There was no statistical difference in post-operative kidney function of the group of patients who had received a combination of carbon dioxide and conventional contrast compared to those that had had conventional contrast alone. This was not what Krassi expected or wanted. Accordingly, he took the data away to reanalyse them himself and returned the next morning with figures showing a clear statistical advantage in favour of the carbon dioxide technique. If there was a valid reason for the different outcome achieved by his analysis, Krassi was not willing to disclose to us what the reason was, and a row ensued. I proposed delaying the submission of any data for presentation or publication anywhere until we had sufficient numbers for more reliable statistical analysis. Krassi did not agree and made clear he was going to submit the abstract to the Vascular Society. At the time it was policy for everyone in the unit who had contributed to research to be named in all related publications and presentations. In this case, because I doubted the ethics, I refused to allow by name to be included. Relations between Krassi and me took a further turn, for the worse.

Yet another major impediment to team cohesion was the thorny issue of private practice. One of the things that really struck me about London, after I arrived, was how much it was driven by money and the pursuit of money. The contrast to Liverpool, where there was so little money, was stark. UCLH is a short walk away from Harley Street, Devonshire Street and the cluster of celebrated private hospitals in Marylebone. There were notable exceptions but it was the norm for UCLH consultants of all specialities, vascular included, to spend a proportion of their time there. Medical private practice, like other commercial enterprises, is a competitive business. The escalating cost of specialist equipment has been a driver behind the formation of cooperative groups but most individuals within these groups continue to practice independently of each other. Genuine teamwork is rare and this limits the scale and complexity of the procedures that tend to be undertaken. All the UCLH vascular consultants, surgeons, radiologists and anaesthetists were engaged in private practice, without any formal arrangement for cooperation between them. Varicose veins operations were, by far, the biggest money-spinner, being quick and easy, mostly complication-free and highly lucrative.

It seemed to me that private practice was another factor that seriously undermined commitment to the vascular project. However, I recognised also that it was not going to go away. So, after giving the matter lots of thought, I came up with a plan to actively engage with private practice in way that I believed could actually strengthen cohesion within the team. We would form a private company to undertake the same complex endovascular work in private as we did in the NHS.

It was a radical idea but I genuinely thought it could work. As one of a very small number of centres throughout the world, able to offer minimally invasive endovascular treatment of highly complex aneurysms and, given our location in London, we were well placed to attract wealthy patients with complex life-threatening aortic aneurysms from around the world. We would be competing on an international scale with a few other big centres in Europe and the United States. The Cleveland Clinic model was a particularly excellent one to follow. In order to realise this vision, there were two basic requirements; first, appropriate facilities and secondly, the support of the team.

It would have been ideal to undertake both our NHS and private work at UCLH. However, this was quickly ruled out. It was not just a matter of space. Strong antipathy towards private practice amongst a substantial number of NHS staff ensured that the small number of private patients already accommodated there were mostly made to feel unwelcome. This was not the sort of ambiance, wealthy patients used to first-class luxury, expected and it would not do. Next, I approached The London Clinic, one of the biggest and best-established private hospitals, just a few minutes down the Marylebone Road from UCLH. The CEO was interested. In fact, he was very interested. I explained that we would require specialised operating equipment, which the hospital did not possess. This was quickly dismissed as an obstacle. Within a very short time, the Executive Board approved a budget of 5 million pounds for construction of a brand-new hybrid operating theatre. This sum was five times more than the cost of the new hybrid theatre, we had built at UCLH. I was invited, and agreed, to chair a Clinical Working Group to advise on its design and provisioning.

So far so good, but I still had to persuade my colleagues of the merits of the plan. It needed everyone on-board if it was to go ahead. Krassi was actually reasonably supportive, at least initially. He had strong associations with The Cleveland Clinic and knew how it could work. Chris was less certain. He was willing to go along with the idea but warned that money tended to have a corrosive effect on interpersonal relationships which, in our case, were not great to start with. Toby, who had lost no time in setting himself up in private practice and was doing well in the varicose veins market, was non-committal. This was not unexpected given his ostracisation from the complex aneurysm programme. Obi was unequivocally opposed. He saw it as an attempt by me, to enrich myself at everybody else's expense. I had not expected Chris's prediction about the corrosive effect of money to be realised quite so soon! I decided to press on anyway. I consulted a commercial lawyer and Heads of Agreement for formation of a limited company were drawn up and circulated. Obi rejected the document out-of-hand and remained implacably opposed. There was no changing his mind. He gave me no choice. Either everybody was in or nobody would be in. I gave up on the idea and paid off the lawyers. Everybody continued with their own independent private practices as before and, having established a good relationship with The London Clinic I started to do a bit myself – not varicose veins!

Although I failed to deliver a team to undertake endovascular treatment of complex aortic aneurysms in wealthy international patients at The London Clinic, as promised, the hospital pressed on with their investment plan nevertheless and I followed through on my commitment to assist them. The end result was a truly fantastic, futuristic state-of-the art hybrid vascular operating facility to rival any in the world. It was opened with a fanfare of publicity just after I had departed from UCLH and London and I never got to use it myself.

In the summer of 2010, the next stage of the process for implementation of the vascular surgery rationalisation programme was getting underway. In North Central London, the Commissioning Authority, acting on behalf of GP's, invited all interested hospitals to submit bids and a senior consultant neurologist, whose name was Nick Losseff, was appointed as an independent non-partisan arbitrator to oversee the process. I was content with this arrangement. It seemed transparent and fair. We had many advantages over the Royal Free. In addition to the excellent facilities of a new hospital and excellent transport links at the apex of the sector, UCLH encompassed all the important specialities allied to vascular surgery, which The Free did not, including cardiac surgery at the adjoining Heart Hospital, neurology in the National Hospital for Neurology and Neurosurgery at Queen Square and the North West Central stroke unit on site. The location of the hospital within the heart of the main University College London campus was also a big plus. I was confident that we could put together a very persuasive case to an unbiased assessor.

The process was scheduled to be completed with a view to implementation within 18 months starting from the summer of 2010. Despite the fact that my vision of a world-leading UCLH endovascular surgery service was already starting to crumble, it seemed to me we were in with a good chance and, if our bid was successful, the complex aneurysm programme would be sure to be revitalised.

It was ironic that the people who had supported my appointment because they had feared being subsumed by The Royal Free, my fellow consultants, seemed to be the most serious obstacles to success. Other than Chris Bishop, who remained loyal to the end, they vacillated from the start. Krassi, who had never had any loyalty to UCLH in the first place, was already in the process of defecting. Not surprisingly, all supporting staff, nurses, radiographers, laboratory technicians were dismayed at the prospect of losing vascular surgery and there was consternation also amongst colleagues of other medical and surgical specialities in the hospital that benefited greatly from the presence of vascular surgery on-site.

Geoff Bellingham, the Medical Director, confirmed that the CEO, Sir Robert Naylor, and the executive team were 'full-square' behind the bid and it was agreed that we would put together the strongest case possible. Accordingly, I got to work with Tom Wright, the general manager for vascular surgery. Tom and I started work at UCLH on the same day and suffered a week of incredibly boring induction lectures together. In his 30s with a business degree, he had been in private commerce before deciding on a career in NHS management. I liked him and we got on well together. The more we delved into the statistics and compared the assets at UCLH in terms of its ability to provide a vascular service to the local community with those of the Royal Free, the more confident we became that independent third-party analysis would find in our favour.

It took us nearly 12 months to prepare a first draft document. A very bulky piece of work, which was widely circulated, and approved, internally. Then, with about six months to go to the deadline for submissions, the decision-making process by the Commissioning Authority took a sinister turn. We received a communication from Nick Losseff to say that if the consultant staff of both hospitals and/or the senior executives of both hospitals could agree from which site vascular services should be provided, then, perhaps we will not need to proceed with the process previously envisioned. I smelled a rat! Someone, somewhere had decided that independent third-party analysis, and public scrutiny, of bids might not yield the desired outcome!

I requested an urgent meeting with Sir Robert Naylor and Geoff Bellingham. Sir Robert said there had been no change to the decision-making process and that we would definitely be submitting a bid from UCLH, as planned. He, then, undermined my confidence by requesting an urgent report from me on the benefits to the hospital of retaining vascular services. Was he not already convinced? Anyway, I presented a report to him within a few days, as requested. It included statements by consultants in the other specialities that depended upon us to emphasise the imperative of retaining vascular services on site. Outside, on the wards and in the corridors, rumours were beginning to circulate that the executive was going to ditch us so I asked Geoff Bellingham to address a meeting of our ancillary and nursing staff all of whom were fearful for their futures. He agreed but, his presentation was lukewarm. Lacking in enthusiasm it convinced no one.

Then, Nick Losseff called a meeting of all vascular consultants from all hospitals in the sector for a round table discussion. There were two hospitals other than UCLH and The Royal Free where some vascular work was undertaken and their representatives attended also. This further increased my suspicion that the impartial, third party decision process was being usurped. If the decision rested upon a vote of all the vascular consultants in the Sector, UCLH would lose because we were outnumbered, even if all of our team voted the right way. And, that was, by no means, certain. I did my best to uphold the case for UCLH but as time went by, I was increasingly a lone voice. A week or two before the submission date for bids, a final meeting was held at The Royal Free which was attended by the senior executives of the two hospitals in addition to the consultants. Whereas the CEO of The Royal Free made an impassioned plea for his own hospital Sir Robert Naylor remained impartial. After the meeting, I contacted Nick Losseff to ask, for the third or fourth time, if impartial, third party analysis of bids had been abandoned. Again, he said that he expected bids to be submitted from both hospitals.

By this time I had managed to secure a draft of the Royal Free bid document and I retained a tiny glimmer of hope because our bid was definitely superior in terms of both content and presentation. It seemed to me that they had not gone to too much trouble to prepare their case and it occurred to me that might be because they were confident of a decision in their favour in any case. They had good cause but, right to the end, I stupidly held on to the hope that a truly independent committee representative of local GPs would recognise that UCLH had a better case and decide accordingly. And, they may well have done had they had the opportunity to do so.

The deadline for submission of bids was 4.00 pm on Friday, 2nd December 2011. At five past four, I received a telephone call from Geoff Bellingham.

He told me the bid from UCLH had not been submitted. I could not believe it! "Why not?" I demanded. "I want to speak to the chief executive."

To which, he replied, "I am speaking from the chief executive's office." The game was now well and truly up.

The writing had been on the wall for a long time. I had refused to see it and consequently suffered an enormous sense of ignominious betrayal. I have no doubt that there had been a clear plan to secure vascular services for UCLH at the start when it was known that the NHS rationalisation programme axe would fall on North Central London. But, sometime afterwards, the plan changed. No one thought to tell me. Or perhaps they did and simply decided not to. Looking back I suspect that the about-turn occurred as far back as 2009, when UCLH was chosen by the NHS to be one of two hospitals in the UK to benefit from a multimillion-pound Proton Beam Accelerator for radiation treatment of cancer. The other site chosen was the Christie Hospital in Manchester. I recall that, when he proudly announced this achievement, Sir Robert Naylor, declared that his ambition, was now to make UCLH the premier hospital for cancer in the UK. I suspect that vascular surgery ceased to have any priority in his mind from that point onwards. I learned subsequently, that the fate of vascular services in North Central London had been sealed finally in a deal made behind closed doors between the CEOs of the two hospitals. A trade was agreed whereby UCLH vascular services would be exchanged for head and neck cancer services that would transfer to UCLH from The Free. No doubt, it was very helpful to the CEOs to have a majority of vascular consultants in their favour but even so, they could not take the risk of an impartial independent committee making the wrong decision. Therefore, transparency and public scrutiny had to be sabotaged.

I am very aware of my own failings in this sorry tale, the most obvious being that of securing the confidence of colleagues and my inability to persuade them of my vision. Dysfunction in the vascular team will not have encouraged Sir Robert Naylor to back our bid, but all of this was almost certainly irrelevant to the final outcome. Had I managed to penetrate the seat of power in the higher administrative circles of the hospital where the decisions were made, I might have had a better idea about what was going on. It would not have changed the outcome, but I would have known that I was wasting my time, and valuable years of my life, fighting battles that I could never win, sooner rather than later. I had been well and truly screwed on all fronts.

The day following my very brief telephone conversation with Geoff Bellingham, I submitted my letter of resignation to Sir Robert Naylor and made my plans to quit the NHS, this time for good.

Chapter 15
Stanley Jackson

Stanley Jackson and his wife, Jean, were returning from their summer holiday in France. Jean had a fear of flying. When the kids were young, they used to go by car but now the two of them preferred Eurostar. They lived up North so took connecting Virgin West Coast trains to and from London. Their annual adventure began and ended at Piccadilly Station in Manchester.

On this occasion, the Eurostar train from Paris was ten minutes late getting into St. Pancras Station and they had dashed up the road to nearby Euston Station dragging their heavy suitcases behind them to catch the Manchester train. They could have taken a taxi but it was not far and they thought running would be quicker. As they paused to catch their breath, on the concourse at Euston Station, Stanley cried out in pain and fell to the floor, his face deathly pale beneath his holiday tan.

UCLH is just a few hundred meters from Euston Station. Within 15 minutes, he was being rushed into the A&E Department and half an hour after that, I was called to review his CT scans, which showed haemorrhage spreading from a huge aneurysm in his belly. Another three hours later, he was recovering from his operation on the vascular ward with a cup of tea, his ruptured aneurysm having been repaired with an endograft under local anaesthetic; no big incision, no blood and no drama. Stanley had been awake and chatting away throughout the operation. Five days later, he was back at Euston station to resume his journey home.

As I headed for home in Hertfordshire on the train from Marylebone station following Stanley's operation I was reminded of another occasion 20 years previously, driving home in the wind and rain along the Dock Road in Liverpool in the early hours of a cold November morning. The thought that had obsessed me at that time was that there had to be a better way than the blood-and-guts surgery that Tom Skully had suffered in his final hours. There was and there is and, though he did not know it, Stanley Jackson was just one lucky beneficiary. In earlier times he would not have had such an easy passage. Since the turn of the millennium there have been many others like him and there will be many more to come. Life today is better for vascular surgeons as well as for their patients. Population screening for aortic aneurysms and the creation of regional teams in place of single-handed vascular surgeons have rendered the unrelenting influx of patients with ruptured aneurysms arriving at all times of the day and night, which was my lonely lot at Broadgreen hospital in the 80s and 90s, a thing of the past. A nightmare no longer experienced by today's generation of vascular surgeons.

Stanley's was the very last operation I ever performed and it was fittingly emblematic of how far everything had changed since my first tentative steps into the world of vascular surgery. I realise that one person's professional lifetime does not count for very much in the grand scheme of things and I absolutely do not claim that there was anything special about mine. But for a miniscule unit of time I had the best possible good fortune to hitch a ride along a never-ending journey of discovery. Who knows where it will lead? Perhaps all surgery, except for trauma, will become a thing of the past as a result of genomics and other, as yet unknown and unimagined, new technologies.

In 1979, when I was first appointed to a consultant post, neither I, nor any of my contemporaries, could ever have possibly imagined treating a ruptured aortic aneurysm through a needle puncture in the groin under local anaesthetic. But, this is now a reality. And, the technological ingenuity that made it possible makes conceivable that which was utterly inconceivable in the early days – vascular surgery with NO MORE BLOOD.

Epilogue

Since writing this book the world has moved on, as it does. Developments have occurred in respect of UK national politics, the NHS and the esoteric world of vascular surgery to which events related in this book are germane and warrant brief additional comment.

On 23rd June 2016, the people of the UK voted in a referendum to leave the European Union. As someone who believed passionately, and still does, in the principles upon which the EU is based and has worked actively to promote and facilitate the freedom of movement of surgeons between member states, I was devastated. It is not the place here to extol the merits of the EU, as the greatest trading block and most successful peace project in history, but I do claim undeniable benefit from the small contribution I and others made to facilitate the free exchange of ideas, expertise and people in the arcane world of vascular surgery. The NHS gained considerably from this and similar exercises in other specialities for a time but, sadly, no longer. Our work is not entirely wasted, far from it. Physicians and surgeons and the healthcare systems of the remaining twenty-seven member states of the EU continue to reap the rewards.

On 12th October 2016, the results, after fifteen years of follow-up, of the UK EVAR 1 Trial (Endovascular versus open repair of abdominal aoric aneurysms) were published in The Lancet. Over this period of 15 years there were marginally more deaths in the patients who had been treated with endovascular repair. Some deaths were related to their aneurysmal disease because aortas that have dilated to form an aneurysm may continue to dilate after treatment but there was also a slightly higher incidence of death related to cancer, which raises questions about the radiation exposure associated with endovascular repair. There may be remedies to address these issues but the main point to be made about the mortality statistics is that death associated with the operation itself is much more likely with open repair than with endovascular repair. And, if you were to ask patients whether they would prefer a slightly higher risk of dying sooner or later there can be little doubt that most would chose the latter. For this reason endovascular repair is popular with patients. However, NICE (National Institute for Health and Care Excellence), in response to the Lancet publication decided that endovascular repair would no longer be approved for elective treatment of abdominal aortic aneurysms. This preposterous decision, which is being challenged by the Vascular Society and others on behalf of the vascular surgical community and patients, is, to my mind at least, a clear demonstration of the negative impact of increasingly centralised micromanagement of healthcare upon the welfare patients. These are surely decisions to be entrusted to individual doctors, about individual patients, based upon knowledge and experience.

From time to time I reflect upon the disturbing events of my final years in the NHS at UCLH. I did not handle situations well and, to a large extent, I was the victim of my own misjudgements, but I have no real regrets. I could have stepped back and left Krassi to his own devices. In which case the disastrous early results of the complex aneurysm programme would have been buried, literally, and the traumas and conflicts associated with its suspension would have been avoided. I do not believe this would have prevented the regional vascular unit locating to The Royal Free at the expense of UCLH but the inevitable would have occurred with considerably less discord and anguish than actually transpired. When these events come back to haunt me I console myself with the conviction that temporary suspension the complex aneurysm programme was absolutely the right decision to make, despite the angst and humiliation that rained down upon me as a consequence. It was a pity, and an indictment upon the systems in place for safeguarding of patients, that I did not get the backing and support that was warranted.

Finally, along with everyone else I am currently confined at home because of the Covid-19 virus pandemic. Many people are dying and it is terrible. However, surprising good can arise from even the darkest of circumstances and this modern plague is bringing about a reappraisal of who and what are really of most value in society. In the Prologue I wrote that the 70 years of the existence of the NHS could turn out to be no more than a transient experiment in socialised medicine. We are now seeing a renaissance of the NHS as a result of Covid-19, which, with a bit of luck, will ensure that the principle of healthcare free at the point of delivery upon which it was founded will remain secure, for a little longer, at least.